Light Battle Cruisers
And
The Second Battle of Heligoland Bight

Lord Fisher's Oddities

Hugh Harkins

[signature] Meadows

December 2015

ISBN: 1-903630-52-5
ISBN-13: 978-1-903630-52-5

Light Battle Cruisers
And
The Second Battle of Heligoland Bight

© Hugh Harkins 2015

Published by Centurion Publishing
Glasgow
United Kingdom

ISBN 10: 1-903630-52-5
ISBN 13: 978-1-903630-52-5

This volume first published in 2015

The Publisher and Author would like to thank all organisations and services for their assistance and contributions in the preparation of this publication

CONTENTS

INTRODUCTION

The naval engagement often referred to as the 'Second Battle of Heligoland Bight', fought on 17 November 1917, between elements of the British Grand Fleet and elements of the German High Seas Fleet, is often sidelined from history. While not being the major clash of fleets like the 'Battle of Jutland' the previous year, or a decisive victory for one side or the other as was the case with the 'Battle of Heligoland Bight' in August 1914, or indeed the battles of 'Coronel' and the 'Falkland Islands' in November and December 1914 respectively, it is significant in being the last naval battle of the war in which capital ships of the opposing British Grand Fleet and the German High Seas Fleet were engaged. Perhaps of more significance, this was the only time that Lord Fisher's controversial 'oddities', the Light Battle Cruisers of the Renown and Courageous Classes engaged enemy warships in battle during the war.

Never, perhaps, in the annals of naval history has there been more controversial Classes of vessels, particularly with the Courageous Class and the unique HMS *Furious*. Often referred to as Battle Cruisers, Lord Fisher, and the Admiralty, referred to them as Light Battle Cruisers, while the Courageous Class became known as Large Light Cruisers, an epitaph attacked after the war, while the Renown Class were simply referred to as Battlecruisers, and the *Furious* was completed as a quasi-aircraft carrier. In his own writings Lord Fisher stated that he was considered "senile and autocratic" for pushing ahead with the Light Battle Cruisers, or "Monstrous Cruisers" as they had been labelled in some areas of Parliament.

This volume sets out to describe the Light Battle Cruisers genesis and briefly outline their development and fielding in the years immediately before the action of 17 November 1917. Chapter 3 details the Second Battle of Heligoland Bight from both the German and British viewpoints, drawing on references from operational documents to support the fact that the oft-stated engagement between HMS *Repulse* and two German Dreadnought Battleships did not actually take place, dispelling the myth that such an engagement took place during the battle; a myth that has endured for almost 100 years.

Many Admiralty Documents were produced with various nomenclature for describing Squadrons or Flotillas, such as 'First Battle Cruiser Squadron' or '1st Battle Cruiser Squadron'. The nomenclature chosen for this volume is 1st rather than First with a few exceptions. It should also be noted that specifications for various vessels changed on the drawing board and during construction, with other changes introduced in service, resulting in many documents being produced with conflicting figures.

Chapter 1 draws on abbreviated text from 'British Battlecruisers of World War 1, an Operational Log', 2013.

1

THE BIRTH OF THE BATTLE CRUISERS

The catastrophic blowing up and sinking of three British Battlecruisers at the Battle of Jutland on 31 May 1916 sealed the British Battlecruisers epitaph in naval history. Flawed designs that should not have been built; words that have echoed through almost one hundred years of history. The seeds of this flawed premise were firmly sown that fateful day that saw the tragic loss of the ships, and almost to a man, their ships complements. Yet these ships were lost in a line of battle engagement and not in the type of action that they were designed for; engaging enemy light forces and Cruisers *ala* the 'Battle of Heligoland Bight' on 28 August 1914, when several German Light Cruisers and Torpedo Boat Destroyers were sunk, and 'The Battle of The Falklands Islands' in December 1914, when the Invincible Class Battlecruisers HMS *Invincible* and *Inflexible* sank the German Armoured Cruisers SMS *Scharnhorst* and *Gneisenau* – these being the operational scenarios envisioned for the Battlecruiser way back in 1906 when they were still being referred to as 'All-Big-Gun Armoured Cruisers'. Volumes could be filled with the tactics and scenarios envisioned for this new class of warship, which would effectively be the bridge between the lumbering, slow, line of Battle Ship to the fast Battleships that could keep pace with, and in some cases, overhaul Light Cruisers, and the later 1920's Class of Warship, the Heavy Cruiser. In this respect then, Lord Fisher's controversial Battle Cruisers had proven to be a success. The losses at Jutland were caused by the ships being in the line of Battle for which they lacked armour protection, and because of flawed practices in the handling and storing of cordite charges.

Towards the end of the 19th Century and in the first few years of the 20th Century, the two power standard that the Royal Navy was being prepared for was in most circles considered to be war with France and Russia in an Alliance. With the Entente Cordial between Britain and France in 1904 this seemed far less likely, but new enemies were emerging with Germany and the United States of America both vying for second place in the naval power ranks, a position which France was fast relinquishing. History has shown that Germany took the number two sea power position, with the United States taking third place. For Britain, a real threat would emerge with a German-United States Alliance. It was evident within the British establishment that "evanescent quarrels" with the United States were likely in the future, and that a "parricidal war" with the United States could not be ruled out as that young nation had many territorial ambitions; some of which would inevitably bring her into conflict with the British Empire if she were to act on them, not least her long standing plans to invade and subjugate the self-Governing Dominion of Canada.

Japan, which was a fast rising naval power in the Far East, had an alliance with Great Britain, which would have a constraining effect on any ambitions the United States may have harboured about becoming involved in a confrontation between Britain and any other major power. However, it was Lord Fisher's belief, not without foundation, that of the three largest naval powers following Britain; France, Germany and the United States, that any combination of two of these powers "would hesitate" to attack Britain, such was Britain's naval supremacy in the first few years of the new Century. He went on to state that if any combination of two of these powers had attacked Britain, then "they would have been defeated" by British Naval Power without "the assistance of our Japanese allies." That said, while confident in British naval supremacy at that time, Lord Fisher's writings make it clear that he was aware that the future of that supremacy would be under threat by the growing naval strength of other naval powers on both sides of the Atlantic.

Lord Fisher had been appointed First Sea Lord on 21 October 1904, under Lord Shelburne's administration, remaining in office for five years and three months. On the same date he was appointed First Sea Lord, he was also appointed First and Principal Naval Aide-de-Camp to King Edward VII. He retired as First Sea Lord on 25 January 1910, succeed by Admiral of the Fleet, Sir Arthur Wilson.

In the first few years of the 20th Century, a revolution was taking place in the design of Capital Ships, leading to the December 1906 launch of HMS *Dreadnought*, the first of the new "all-big-gun" Capital ships, which would be colloquially known from that time onwards as Dreadnoughts.

A memorandum 'Admiralty Work and Progress', issued by the then First Lord, Lord Cawdor, on 30 November 1905, stated "At the present time strategic requirements necessitate an output of four large armoured ships annually." An announcement in Parliament in July 1906 stated that only three Battleships (Cawdor's large armoured ships) were to be included in the then current program. Among the reasons cited for withdrawal from the planned four Battleships was that there had been a temporary halt in Battleships construction on the Continent of Europe following the advent of HMS *Dreadnought*, the first all-big-gun Battleship, and the planned Invincible Class 'all-big-gun Armoured Cruisers' (these vessels had not yet been designated Battle Cruiser). Foreign navies had been forced to revaluate their construction programs to compete with the revolutionary new type of Battleship, which was not only much heavier armed, but in most areas better armoured and several knots faster than the existing status quo vessels which would soon have the indignation of being labeled 'Pre-Dreadnought' Battleships.

The reduction from four to three Battleships caused much disquiet among certain circles within the establishment, particularly as it came so soon after the ascension to power of the new Liberal government, who were being outright accused of jeopardising the security of the United Kingdom. At the time of this memorandum, the assumption within press circles was that only two of these ships were to be Battleships and two Armoured Cruisers. It has to be remembered though that at this time there was no public conception of what the Invincible Class actually was (they would later be termed Battle Cruisers) and the general fallback description within the press was that they were modern Armoured Cruisers. Fisher saw these vessels very differently; more of a fast Battleship, as borne out by his writings "… with its 6 knots superiority of speed to everything afloat, and the biggest guns alive. The *Invincible's* are as a matter of fact, perfectly fit to be in the line of battle with the battle fleet, and could more correctly be described as battleships, which thanks to their speed, can drive anything afloat off the seas.

"Panic at the present time is stupid. The Board of Admiralty is not to be frightened by paper programs. They will cautiously do all that they judge necessary to secure the existing naval supremacy of this country: the moment that is threatened they will throw caution to the winds and out build our rivals at all costs".

The name sake of the first of the new class of ship that would eventually become known as the Battle Cruiser or Battlecruiser (Battle Cruiser was the official tern), HMS *Invincible,* was ordered in 1906, laid down at the Armstrong Elswick Works Ltd shipyard in Newcastle-upon-Tyne on 2 April 1906, and launched just over a year later on 13 April 1907. She was commissioned on 20 March 1909, but was not the first of the new 'Large Armoured Cruisers' to be completed; HMS *Indomitable* and HMS *Inflexible* having commissioned in June and October the previous year respectively. *Indomitable*, ordered in 1906, as the second of the three *Invincible* Class, was laid down at Fairfield Shipbuilding and Engineering Company at Govan Shipyard on the River Clyde on 1 March 1906, launched on 16 March 1907, and commissioned on 1 June 1908 (some sources claim she was commissioned on 20 June 1908). The third of the Invincible Class, HMS *Inflexible*, was laid down at John Brown shipyard on the Clyde on 5 February 1906, launched on 26 June 1907 and Commissioned at Chatham on 20 October 1908.

HMS *Invincible* (top) was the namesake of the three first generation Battlecruisers of the Invincible Class. The second Generation Battlecruisers of the Indefatigable Class depicted by HMAS *Australia* (above) were little more than improved variants of the Invincible Class, featuring the same main armament, albeit with a different arrangement for the wing turrets which were staggered to allow all eight 12-in guns to be fired in a broadside. BO and LOC

Following on from the three Invincible Class, three Indefatigable Class Battle Cruisers were ordered, one of which would enter service with the fledgling RAN (Royal Australian Navy), while the remaining two would be commissioned into the Royal Navy; one of these, HMS *New Zealand*, being paid for by the self-governing Dominion of New Zealand after which the ship was named. The Indefatigable Class were larger and heavier than the proceeding Invincible Class, but retained the 8 x 12-in gun main armament, although the arrangement was altered from that of the Invincible Class.

The first of the three Indefatigable Class, HMS *Indefatigable*, was laid down on 23 February 1909, launched on 28 October that year and commissioned at Devonport on 24 February 1911. HMS *New Zealand*, was ordered in 1909, laid down at Fairfield Shipbuilding Company on the River Clyde on 20 June 1910, launched on 1 July 1911, and commissioned in 1912. The third and last of the Indefatigable Class, HMAS *Australia*, was ordered to be built by John Brown and Company in March 1910, laid down on 26 June 1910, and launched on 25 October 1911. HMAS *Australia* was to form the centerpiece of the RAN, being the only capital ship in service with the young naval arm when she commissioned at Portsmouth on 21 June 1913.

The first of the Lion Class Battlecruisers, HMS *Lion*, was laid down at Devonport dockyard on 25 November 1909, launched on 6 August 1910, and commissioned on 4 June 1912. Larger than her predecessors of the Indefatigable Class, HMS *Lion's* displacement was some 26,250 tons standard and 29,680 tons at full load, and she was the first Battle Cruiser to adopt the 13.5-in gun primary armament with superimposed forward 'A' and 'B' turrets.

Lions sister ship, HMS *Princess Royal*, was laid down at Vickers Yard on 2 May 1910, launched on 24 April (some records suggest 29 April) 1911, completed in October 1912 and commissioned at Devonport on 12 November that year.

Following the two *Lion* Class, the Admiralty ordered a modified vessel, which was named HMS *Queen Mary*. This vessel is often described as a separate or sub-class from the *Lion* Class – rightly so since the differences are quite considerable in some areas. HMS *Queen Mary*, the only one of her type, was ordered to be built at Palmers in the 1910 building program, laid down on 6 March 1911, launched on 20 March 1912, and commissioned on 4 September 1913.

Initially HMS *Tiger* was planned as a fourth unit of the Lion Class incorporating the same modifications as the third Unit, HMS *Queen Mary*. However, she was completely redesigned to become the sole vessel of the improved Tiger Class as a result of design experience gained in development of the Kongo Class Battle Cruisers designed by Vickers chief designer Sir George Thurston for the Japanese Navy, the first of which IJN *Kongo* was laid down by Vickers-Armstrong on 17 January 1911. HMS *Tiger* was laid down on 20 June 1912, launched on 15 December 1913, and completed and commissioned in October 1914.

The third generation Battlecruisers of the Lion Class, depicted by HMS *Princess Royal* (top), was a vast improvement on the previous vessels of the Invincible and Indefatigable Classes, being faster, better armed, and with increased armour protection. The sole vessel of the Tiger Class, HMS *Tiger* (above) improved on the Lion Class, introducing a 6-in anti-torpedo boat armament and better protection. LOC and RN

During their respective service careers there were a number of reports that the four 'Cats' known as the 'Splendid Cats', *Lion, Princess Royal, Queen Mary* and *Tiger*, attained 30 knots, but it is doubtful that any of them other than the *Tiger* actually managed this speed, even for a brief period.

'Speed is armour' was Lord Fisher's Maxim. In the new class of warship, which became known as the Battle Cruiser, armour protection was sacrificed for firepower and speed. In contrast, the German Battle Cruisers were more heavily armoured than their British counterparts, achieved at the cost of a knot or two of speed in comparison to their respective British counterparts. Despite this slightly inferior speed of the German vessels, the British Battle Cruisers were never able to overhaul the German vessels before they had reached the safety of their fortified harbours. As an example: with a ship at maximum speed of 24 knots with a 20 mile start over a 28 knot vessel it would take at least five hours to close to within effective gun range of 10 miles, during which a distance of around 130 miles would be covered during a stern chase, which would be typical of the North Sea war. In reality the North Sea simply proved to be too small for such scenarios to result in the successful running down of the German Battle Cruisers before the latter were back in the safety of their fortified anchorages. Thereby, looking back it could be said that the Germans had the major advantage of heavy armour, which saved several vessels from destruction, but the British were rarely able to gain from their advantage of superior speed.

The need for ever faster capital ships was not lost in other areas of the Admiralty. The following text from a speech by Admiral Sir Reginald Bacon at a meeting of the Institution of Naval Architects on 12 March 1913 shows the mood of the time: "I quite see from one point of view that to lose two guns for an extra five-knot speed seems a great loss; but there is one question which I should like to ask, and that is whether you would send out to sea a whole fleet, the whole strength of the nation, with no single ship of sufficient superior speed to pick up a particular ship of the enemy? That is the point to rivet your attention upon. We must always in our Navy have ships of greatly superior speed to any one particular ship in the enemy's fleet, otherwise over the face of the sea you will have ships of the enemy roaming about that we cannot overhaul and that nothing can touch."

In some areas of the pre-war Admiralty, Fisher was regarded as a 'madman' and Winston Churchill was disliked immensely, particularly within the Navy itself; considered to be rude, particularly if criticised. Churchill regarded Fisher as a genius, but a genius who had to be controlled, while Fisher saw Churchill as nothing more than a political figure and treated him as such; fighting him on some issues while supporting him on others. For instance, Fisher had long supported Churchill's selection of Jellico as commander of the Grand Fleet. The appointment of the commander of the 2nd Battle Cruiser Squadron, which was opposed by Beatty (who commanded the Battle Cruiser Squadron – later Fleet, under the overall command of Jellicoe, Commander-in-Chief of the Grand

Fleet), who was not consulted, was supported by both Lord Fisher and Churchill. It was accepted that Fisher and Beatty disliked each other. As early as 1912, it had become clear to observers that Beatty disliked Fisher and Vis a Vis, Fisher disliked Beatty. It is assumed that their mutual dislike was from reputation as when Beatty was favourably mentioned to Fisher in conversation in 1912, he merely replied "Really? Never met him".

While presiding over the Royal Commission on Oil Fuel and Oil, a post he took up on 30 July 1912, Fisher had a vision of Britain's large fleet of warships, particularly the Battle Cruisers, dominating the seas by remaining on station for long periods, refueling at sea when required. His view was that there would be millions of tons of oil fuel always at sea on tankers in transit from port to port. Wireless stations would plot the position of every tanker and all the warships would have to do was intercept them and refuel. While this theory was not realised during the 1914-1918 war, it was a vision of the future and during the Second World War it would be practiced by most of the major naval powers to some degree or other with the United States Navy in particular employing large 'Fleet Trains' to support its drive across the Pacific Ocean.

Pre-war doctrine outlined two main functions for the Battlecruisers.
1. Scout ahead of the main Battle Fleet and
2. To act as either bait or a provocation to try and entice the enemy battle fleet (always considered to be the German Fleet) to come out and engage them, thereby drawing them onto the guns of the British Battle Fleet.

In addition, 1913 doctrine saw the Battle Cruiser Squadron being used in conjunction with the Light Cruiser Squadrons to conduct reconnaissance of enemy coastlines, support blockading forces or Armoured Cruiser patrols, to act as support between blockading forces and the Battle Fleet when the latter was at sea, and supporting a Cruiser force at sea when tasked to watch an enemy fleet.

Despite being much weaker in armour protection compared with contemporary Battleships of the period, the Battlecruisers heavy firepower inevitably meant that an additional role would be to take a place in the line of Battle in a fleet action once the Battle Fleet had become engaged with the enemy. In this role the Battlecruisers would effectively act as a fast division of the Battle Fleet, preferably positioned on one of the flanks.

In the first few years, particularly the first six months, of the war the Battlecruisers were used in a varying degree of roles including some that were not in the 1913 doctrine for their planned wartime role. Many of the duties of the Battlecruisers were controversial and were contested by some as they could as effectively have been conducted by smaller vessels or older Battleships.

2

THE LIGHT BATTLE CRUISERS

While the original Battlecruisers of the Invincible, Indefatigable, Lion and Tiger Classes had their obvious design flaws; mainly in their week armour protection in comparison to their German counterparts, they had proven to be operationally successful, dominating the North Sea and some distant stations throughout the war. The new Light Battle Cruisers (Light Battlecruisers), *Renown* and *Repulse,* were indeed flawed, as their armour protection was little better than that of the Invincible Class of 1906, and much inferior to the Lion, Queen Mary and in particular the Tiger Class. The Courageous Class were even weaker in armour protection than the Invincible Class, being considered little more that modern Light Cruisers armed with a powerful battery of 4 x 15 in guns. These controversial warships were originally laid down under plans for Lord Fisher's Baltic Project, which required some 600 or so low draught vessels capable of entering the shallow waters of the Baltic Sea to support a Russian landing on the Pomeranian Coast, thereafter a huge Russian Army could march on Berlin and end the War in 1915; all theoretical of course. However, this project was ultimately cancelled, although some vessels were completed with some modifications, including the Courageous Class and *Furious* Light Battlecruisers, which although not as low in draught as they had been planned to be, were certainly lower than Capital Ships of the time, which it was contended would allow then to follow German Light Forces retreating into shallow coastal waters; areas which had previously been off limits to heavy caliber gun ships such as Battlecruisers and Battleships.

Almost one hundred years on from their introduction to service, the Light Battlecruisers still stir up intense debate. The Admiralty is often labelled foolhardy for introducing the *Renown* and *Repulse* to the 1st Battle Cruiser Squadron. However, it has to be remembered that these were immensely powerful warships, their weakness being in their armour protection. Their introduction to service as fully fledged Battlecruisers stemmed from several main points. Firstly, the Battle of Jutland on 31 May 1916 had resulted in the loss three British Battlecruisers – a first generation Battlecruisers of the Invincible Class, HMS *Invincible*, a second generation Battlecruiser of the Indefatigable Class, HMS *Indefatigable*, and a third generation Battlecruiser, the unique HMS *Queen Mary*. The loss of these three powerful warships constituted a reduction by almost a third of the then available British Battlecruiser force, leaving only seven available vessels, HMS *Indomitable* and HMS *Inflexible* of the Invincible Class, HMS *New Zealand* and HMAS *Australia* of the Indefatigable Class, HMS *Lion* and *Princess Royal* of the Lion Class and HMS *Tiger*, sole vessel of the Tiger Class. As the Grand Fleet was active in the North Sea, the weaker German fleet, rightly, refusing action while the scales were tipped so heavily against it, it was assumed that a general action between the Grand Fleet and the German High Seas fleet would take place only at a time of the German choosing, which would probably be when at least one British Battlecruiser was undergoing refit, reducing the British force to only six vessels.

The importance of the Battlecruiser in the Royal Navy at this time cannot be overstated. Based at Rosyth on the River Forth, they, with their high speed, were the only capital ships with any realistic chance of intercepting a German raiding force of Battlecruisers and Light Cruisers attempting to bombard British East Coast Towns and ports, the main body of the Grand Fleet being nominally based further north at Scapa Flow in the Orkney Islands, there being no suitable East Coast ports capable of housing the bulk of the Grand Fleet. Likewise, any serious disruption of a German invasion force in the early stages of an invasion, a very real, if reduced, threat in 1916/1917, would be reliant on the British Battlecruisers. The shortage of available Battlecruisers meant that there was no question of the *Renown* and *Repulse*, at least, not joining one or other of the Battle Cruiser Squadrons, despite their weakness in armour protection.

Even with the addition of *Renown* and *Repulse*, the Admiralty still considered the Battlecruiser Force to be much too week for the roles it was tasked with. In August 1917, the Admiralty appreciation of the opposing Battlecruisers fleets was thus: The stronger portion of the fleet included the three remaining 'Cats', HMS *Lion*, HMS *Princess Royal* and HMS *Tiger*. These vessels were considered to be inferior to the German Derfflinger Class Battlecruisers, SMS *Derfflinger* and SMS *Hindenburg* (this latter vessel commissioned in summer 1917).

The weaker group consisted of HMS *New Zealand*, HMAS *Australia*, HMS *Renown*, HMS *Repulse*, HMS *Inflexible* and HMS *Indomitable*. These vessels were grouped against the German Battlecruisers SMS *Seydlitz*, SMS *Moltke* and SMS *Von Der Tann*. Of these, the First Lord of the Admiralty remarked that "Renown and Repulse are absolutely outclassed by and not fit even to engage the Manteuffel and Hindenburg: that Tiger and Derfflinger, Princess Royal, Lion and Seydlitz are fairly matched except for very inadequate torpedo protection in our (British) ships: that New Zealand and Australia are badly outclassed by Moltke: and that Inflexible and Indomitable are considerably inferior to Von der Tann in protection and speed, though somewhat superior in armament…" The Admiralty also concluded that the German Battlecruisers, "as well as being much superior in protection and that their guns have considerably greater range than the British… In speed the slowest German Battle Cruiser exceeds by two knots our slowest, so that they can draw our fast ships ahead of the slower ones."

The Admiralty expected another German Battlecruiser, erroneously named Manteuffel (mentioned above), to commission within a few months and expected SMS *Mackensen*, the first of the Mackensen Class, to commission in November 1918, while the Admiral Class Battlecruiser, HMS *Hood*, the next planned British Battlecruiser, was, at that time, expected to commission about December 1918. To make the Admiralty's headache worse, as previously stated, it was expected that a general action in which the opposing Battlecruiser forces would face off would be at a time of the German choosing, which would undoubtedly be when they had all available Battlecruisers in commission, while the British would no doubt have at least one vessel undergoing refit.

For these reasons, in an attempt to alleviate the crisis of available Battlecruiser numbers, the Admiralty took the unusual step of requesting the War Cabinet to consider attempting to purchase at least two of the Japanese Kongo Class Battlecruisers, which were considered to be superior to any of the in service British Battlecruisers at that time, including the *Tiger*, the design of which stemmed from the design of the Kongo Class.

The text of the following Memorandum brings to the fore the Admiralty's concerns and dismay about the lack of protection in the Renown Class leading to the attempt to purchase Japanese Battlecruisers.

BATTLE CRUISER STRNGTH

Memorandum for the War Cabinet.
by the First Lord of the Admiralty.

"The Board of Admiralty desire to draw the attention of the War Cabinet to the serious situation which will arise by the end of this year in regard to the comparative strength of the British and German Battle Cruiser Forces. Owing to their superiority in armour protection and speed, raids can be carried out with comparative impunity by German Battle Cruisers on our Coasts and East Coast shipping and successful scouting work for the Battle Fleet by the Battle Cruiser Force becomes a matter of considerable difficulty, and places the Battle Fleet at a disadvantage on joining action with the High Sea Fleet. The Board suggest that the only way of meeting this danger is by using Japanese

Battle Cruisers. The Japanese are unlikely to consent to such craft joining the Grand Fleet, and in any case, it is doubtful whether, manned by Japanese, they would be a match for the German Battle Cruisers. The Board suggests for the consideration of the War Cabinet that the Foreign Office should be asked to instruct the Ambassador at Tokio (Tokyo) to sound the Japanese Government as to whether they would sell two Battle Cruisers."

20 August 1917

More than a year later the British had been unable to convince the Japanese to part with any of their Battlecruisers despite the fact that the British Government "had used every effort to obtain these, but with no result."

In truth the Battle Cruiser Force had always been considered too weak for some of the roles is was expected to fulfill. In the case of German raids on the British East coast by the Battlecruisers and Light Cruisers of the Scouting Groups, The Battle Cruiser Fleet, as it was known in 1916, was expected to attempt to intercept the raiding force, probably on its withdrawal. This, however, risked bringing the British Battlecruisers into an engagement with not only the German Battlecruisers, but one or more Squadrons of the High Seas Fleet, which might be in support of the German Battlecruisers. This, it was feared could lead to the annihilation of the Battle Cruiser Fleet before the bulk of the Grand Fleet, steaming from its anchorage at Scapa Flow in the Orkney's far to the north, could reach the scene of the battle. Following the Battle of the Dogger Bank, in which the British sunk the German Battlecruiser (modern Armoured Cruiser) SMS *Blucher*, but suffered extensive damage to the Flagship, HMS *Lion*, Vice-Admiral Beatty, then Commander of the Battle Cruiser Fleet petitioned for the newly emerging 5th Battle Squadron, with its four Queen Elizabeth Class fast Battleships armed with a battery of eight x 15-in guns, to be incorporated into the Battle Cruiser Fleet. Admiral Jellicoe, Commander of the Grand Fleet, argued against this, stating that although the Queen Elizabeth Class had a design speed of 25 knots, comparable with the first generation Battlecruisers of the Invincible Class, they would be capable of only 23 ½ knots until a about 1,000 tons of fuel had been consumed, therefore hindering the Battle Cruiser Fleet if it was forced to retire in the face of the bulk of the High Seas Fleet. He further stated that the Battle Cruiser Fleet, even supported by the 5th Battle Squadron, would have to retire if the German Battle Cruisers were supported by two or more Battle Squadrons. Beatty argued that these vessels, even at 23 ½ knots, would be able to keep station with the Battle Cruiser Fleet until the enemy was sighted. In a chase lasting three hours, he contended, the 5th Battle Squadron would be trailing only some 4 ½ miles astern of the 3rd Battle Cruiser Squadron, and therefore, able to provide valuable heavy support.

HMS *Repulse* being launched on 8 January 1916 (top) and in dock at Clydebank on 13 August 1916 (above).

The debate about whether the 5th Battle Squadron should join the Battle Cruiser Fleet or be retained by Jellicoe at Scapa Flow with the Bulk of the Grand Fleet continued through the remainder of February and March 1916. Various letters and memorandum outlining the pros and cons of such a move went to and thro, however, in the end the 5th Battle Squadron did not join the Battle Cruiser Fleet, although it was often deployed south to Rosyth for operations with the Battle Cruiser Fleet; one such deployment taking place at the end of May 1916, when the 5th Battle Squadron was temporarily attached to, and sailed with, the Battle Cruiser Fleet for its fateful encounter with the High Seas Fleet at the Battle of Jutland on 31 May 1916. The Battle Cruiser Fleet encountered and engaged the German Battlecruisers and Light Cruisers before it was forced to withdraw in the face of the bulk of the German High Seas Fleet. The Battle Cruiser Fleet lost the Battlecruiser HMS *Queen Mary* and HMS *Indefatigable* during the engagement with the German Battlecruisers. Retiring in the direction of approaching Grand Fleet which was steaming southerly, the 5th Battle Squadron took up the rear of the Battle Cruiser Fleet and fought an intense rear-guard action with the High Seas Fleet.

The action on 31 May 1916 leads to the conclusion that both Jellicoe and Beatty were correct to a certain degree. Jellicoe was correct in stating that even with the 5th Battle Squadron in support, the Battle Cruiser Fleet would have to retire in the face of the German Battlecruiser supported by two or more Battle Squadrons. Beatty, however, was correct that even in such a scenario the 5th Battle Squadron would offer invaluable support, which it did at Jutland, taking the brunt of the High Seas Fleet fire for several hours during the so called 'Run to the North' when the Battle Cruiser Fleet steamed in the direction of the Grand Fleet. The weakly armoured vessels of the 3rd Battle Cruiser Squadron, which was with the Grand Fleet at the time, would have suffered severely had it been in the position of the 5th Battle Squadron during the run to the north. One of these vessels, HMS *Invincible*, was blown up later in the day during the general action.

At the post Jutland Conference held at the Admiralty on 24 June 1916, one major question was the future employment of the Queen Elizabeth Class fast Battleships of the 5th Battle Squadron which had proved their value as fast powerful well armoured warships at the Battle of Jutland. Their invaluable support as the rear element of the Battle Cruiser Fleet during the 'Run to the North' stoked up the debate from earlier in the year as to whether they should be a fast wing of the Battle Fleet or an integral part of the Battle Cruiser Fleet. The Admiralty concluded that the 5th Battle Squadron should be "considered mainly as a fast wing division of the battle fleet and not a portion of the Battle Cruiser Fleet." While this appeared to settle once and for all the role of the 5th Battle Squadron, the following caveat was introduced "That occasion may arise when at my discretion I may consider it desirable to reinforce the battle cruisers with the Fifth Battle Squadron, *but they are to be considered simply as a reinforcement, and not in no sense an integral portion of the Battle Cruiser Fleet.*" "The extent to which they are utilised in support of the battle cruisers, and away from the vicinity of the battle fleet, will depend in some degree on the speed which is attained by *Barham* on the measured mile at the mouth of the Clyde during her forthcoming steam trials." HMS *Barham* conducted the steam trials in Bute Sound on 6 July 1916, while on passage from Devonport to Scapa Flow. During the trials she attained a mean speed of 23.9 knots, recorded in the *Barham's* log.

It is, therefore, with the bigger picture of operational commitments and available resources that it can be appreciated that, despite its acceptance that the so called Light Battle Cruisers were vastly inferior to their German opposite numbers in armour protection, they had to be used to shore up numbers of vessels available to the Battle Cruiser Fleet, which was later renamed the Battle Cruiser Force - their being simply no other option other than to cede much of the hard won control of the North Sea to the German Fleet, which, despite the fact that it might not fully exploit such a situation, would have been in a much easier situation in regards to bombardment sorties of the British East Coast or attacks on coastal shipping.

While historical records paint a clearer picture of why it was necessary for *Repulse* and *Renown* to operate as Battlecruisers, they also show that the Admiralty was all too aware of their vulnerability, which was a constant worry throughout the remainder of the war. Perhaps the most damning report on the suitability of the Renown Class as Battlecruisers came in an August 1918 Admiralty Memorandum to the War Cabinet which stated of the *Renown* and *Repulse* "unfortunately these ships are practically unprotected at present., they have only a narrow 6" belt between the Turrets and are… liable to be blown up by the enemy's shell fire."

Renown Class

When Lord Fisher returned to the Admiralty, taking up his post as First Sea Lord on 30 October 1914, as successor to Admiral Louis of Battenberg, no Battlecruisers were under construction to follow HMS *Tiger* which was just completing at that time. He was dismayed to note that the Revenge Class Battleships which were being built to follow the Queen Elizabeth Class 15-in gun Battleships (all of the latter Class were undergoing construction with some close to completion) were an inferior design to their predecessors; being slower and designed for coal and oil burning. Although the Revenge Class would be well armoured, and, Like the Queen Elizabeth Class, armed with a powerful battery of eight 15-in guns, Fisher saw the design as a backward step in the development of the Battle Fleet. In a letter to the Prime Minister he wrote of the Revenge Class "Why this design was adopted I do not know, unless it were for economy."

Once in his position as First Sea Lord and able to bring his weight to bear, Fisher set about trying to remedy some of the shortcomings of the Revenge Class. However, construction of most of the ships ordered was too far advanced to radically change the design, and Fisher was only able to change the Class to oil burning only, removing the outdated coal burning requirement. Even as late as 1916, Fisher thought that this would "considerably improve" the speed of the Class. However, these vessels entered service with the standard 21 knot speed of the previous Classes of Dreadnought Battleships with the exception of the Queen Elizabeth Class, which was capable 25 knots (after burning of a portion of its fuel oil), bringing them close to the speed of the first and second generation Battlecruisers. The Queen Elizabeth Class were remarkable ships for the time and were the first true fast Battleships, as well as being considered the most powerful warships in the world when they entered service, and certainly superior to any Dreadnought into the 1920's. In contrast, the USN for example did not introduce a Battleship faster than 21 knots until 1941.

The two Battlecruisers of the Renown Class were initially planned as the last two 15-in gun Royal Sovereign (later Revenge) Class Battleships. When World War 1 broke out in August 1914, it was initially expected, or at least hoped, that the conflict would be over quickly; the massed armies of the opposing sides clashing in one decisive campaign that would provide victory for one side or the other. However, following the initial German and allied offensives on the Western Front, the opposing sides settled into the stalemate of trench warfare on the European Continent as winter 1914 approached. As it was becoming clear that the war was not going to be over quickly plans for the last two of the planned seven Revenge Class Battleships remained on hold; the vessels which had only just commenced construction, having been suspended on 26 August 1914, as the Admiralty felt it would not be able to bring them into service quickly enough to be of any use in the then current war and required the manpower and resources for its huge build program of light forces such as Minesweepers and Destroyers. However, after Lord Fisher took over as First Sea Lord towards the end of October 1914, he immediately set about an energetic campaign for construction of more Battlecruisers. With little real prospect of getting his hoped for program of three new 15-in gun Battlecruisers approved, Fisher began lobbying Lord of the Admiralty, Winston Churchill, to agree to the redesign of the two cancelled Revenge Class Battleships to Battlecruisers. Much of the materials already procured or sourced, such as gun turrets and guns, could still be used in their construction, reducing costs compared with a completely new design, although this consideration was secondary to the primary consideration of construction timescale. Churchill continued to object as he felt the vessels would not be constructed in sufficient time to be used in the war, which seemed sufficient reason to reject a compromise design whose *raison d'etre* would be to increase Battlecruiser numbers in the, then, current war with Germany. Fisher was, however, able to convince Churchill that with energetic enthusiasm he would get the vessels constructed and in service in similar timescales to that seen with the Dreadnought in 1905/6. Fisher's argument winning through, Churchill agreed to his demands and obtained the approval of the Cabinet on 28 December 1914, allowing work on the vessels to recommence, although now they were to be built as fast 'Light Battle Cruisers', armed with a 15-in main Battery, reduced from eight in the Revenge Class Battleships to six in the new Light Battle Cruisers that would emerge as the Renown Class.

As Fairfield and Palmers, where the two cancelled Revenge Class Battleships were to have been built, lacked slipways large enough for the new Battlecruiser design, the contract for their construction went to John Brown at Clydebank; the vessels being ordered on 30 December 1914, the terms of the contract calling for construction within 15-18 months, although these contracts were apparently not produced until March 1915.

Despite his advancing years; 73 years old, Lord Fisher energetically set about procuring additional materials and manpower for the construction of the two ships, construction of which was indeed hastened with Fisher's policy of thrashing on with getting the ships ready while sorting out the red tape later. Although the plan was for both ships to be completed within 15-18 months, by early 1916 it was becoming clear that *Renown* would not be ready in time, although it looked like her sister, *Repulse*, could be completed within that timeframe.

HMS *Renown* at the Grand Fleet anchorage at Scapa Flow in the Orkney Islands to the north of mainland Scotland. British Official

Top: This photograph apparently shows HMS *Repulse* during acceptance sea trials on 14 August 1916. Above: HMS *Repulse*. British Official

Top: HMS *Repulse* approaching the iconic Forth Rail Bridge in the Firth of Forth, circa 1916-17. Above: HMS *Renown* circa 1916-17. British Official

The two vessels of the Renown Class were named HMS *Renown* and HMS *Repulse*; plans for a third vessel, named HMS *Resistance*, being dropped before any construction work commenced. In designing the new Class, the Basic *Revenge* Class Battleship hull was lengthened and the armour protection of the vessels was considerably reduced to save weight. The four 15-in gun twin turrets were reduced to three to save space and weight further. Reducing the armour protection also reduced the amount of time required to build the ships, therefore, allowing the ships to be brought into service more quickly.

The Renown Class were built with a 6-in (152 mm) armour belt, tapering to 1.5-in (38-mm) at the ends. Deck protection included 1.5-in armour over the forecastle deck, 0.5-in (1.25-cm) over the upper deck, 2.5-in (6.4-cm) over the lower deck, 3.5-in (9-cm) over the steering compartment and 3-in (76-mm) over the main deck. As designed, the barbets included 7-in (18-cm) armour reducing to 4-in (10-cm), the main armament turret front faces were to be 9-in or 11-in, depending on whatever records were in force at the time, and the turret roof was 4.25-in (10.8 cm). The conning tower was protected by 10-in (25-cm) armour and the communications tubes were protected by 3-in (76-mm) armour.

Design weight was 26,500 tons as standard, which would be increased to 31,000+ tons at maximum load (this weight would increase in service). With a length of 794-ft 2.5-in (240-m) overall they were the largest (in terms of length) warships in the world at the time they entered service, and remained so into the 1920's. As designed, the vessels had a Beam of 90-ft and had a normal draught of around 26-27-ft. **Note:** There were several iterations during design and the figures of many will naturally differ from those quoted above.

The larger hull size and reduced armament compared with the Revenge Class Battleships provided the space required for the propulsion machinery, required to produce the high speed necessary for the Battlecruiser role. The 42 Babcock & Wilcox Boilers and Brown Curtis geared steam turbines drove four shafts, producing 112-120,000 SHP (**Note:** figures vary from document to document), translating to a very fast 30.25 knot speed for service use. During sea trials HMS *Renown* achieved a speed of 32.68 knots and her sister, HMS *Repulse,* achieved 31.7 knots. Lord Fisher's vision of producing the fastest Battlecruisers afloat had been realised.

The primary armament consisted of six BL 15-in/.42 Mark I guns housed in three twin turrets; two, 'A' and 'B', forward, and one, 'Y', aft. Secondary armament consisted of seventeen BL 4-in/.44 (102-mm) low angle guns, 2 x 3-in (76-mm) anti-aircraft guns, 4 x 3-pdr guns and 2 x 21-in (533-mm) submerged torpedo tubes. In service, Flying-off platforms were fitted to 'B' and 'Y' turrets enabling the vessels to operate scout aircraft.

Lord Fisher resigned his office as First Sea Lord on 15 May 1915 "over the Dardanelles question" (Fisher resigned over the Gallipoli Campaign for which he had vehemently disagreed with one of the campaigns proponents, Lord of the Admiralty Winston Churchill). On 5 July 1915, he was appointed Chairman of the Board of Invention and Research. Following his resignation as First Sea Lord, he no longer had control over the construction of the Light Battlecruisers, which would soon suffer delays. In his writings in 1916, Lord Fisher stated "Personally, I have always been strongly of the opinion that all the 'Royal Sovereigns' (Revenge) should have been battle cruisers, which are the dominating type of the day." He defended the 'Light Battlecruisers' of the Renown and Courageous Classes, and the oddball *Furious*, by stating that in his opinion "ships of the 'Repulse', 'Courageous' and 'Furious' types were MORE (Fisher's Capitals to emphasize the more) required, at the time and under the conditions when they were commenced, than heavy battle cruisers, especially having in view the rapidity with which they could be finished and in service, whereas the heavier type could not under any circumstances be built in under two years." He went on to say "My views on this point have not changed, and I consider it a calamity that any of these ships have been allowed to fall behind in their dates of delivery."

HMS *Renown* at anchor probably in the Firth of Forth or Scapa Flow, around 1917. BO

In a letter to the Prime Minister, David Lloyd George, in March 1916, Lord Fisher discussed the lack of new heavy Battlecruisers under construction, making clear his dismay and that any shortage of Battlecruisers of the "Lion type", meaning heavy Battlecruisers, by 1916 was the fault of the previous Board of the Admiralty for not ordering more of such vessels prior to 1914, as such vessels, which could be ready in 1916 would have had to have been laid down quite a while before the start of the war in August 1914. He was also clear that from May 1915 he would have "pressed forward the building of battle cruisers of the largest and most heavily armed type" due to the uncertainly that had become apparent as to the duration of the war and the lack of information as regards the building of German Battlecruisers. In short, he justified this position as being prepared for "all eventualities."

HMS *Renown* circa 1917/18. British Official

He noted in his letter that he had a "design of this type (heavy battle cruiser) fully prepared and a model made" just before he left the Admiralty in May 1915. Fisher was in no doubt that the labour for construction of the new class of heavy battle cruiser could have been procured by "energetic action" had orders been "judiciously" placed.

The new heavy Battlecruiser, a sketch and model of which was produced, was colloquially referred to as HMS *Incomparable*, which featured a 20-in main armament. In his writings, Lord Fisher stated of this Class of vessel, "but for the prodigious development of aircraft, would have been as great a New Departure as was the Dreadnought." This showed that Lord Fisher understood the threat aircraft could pose to even the most powerfully armed Capital Ships.

Each of the new designs 20-in guns weighed in at around 200 tons and fired a projectile weighing 2 tons, which would reach a height of over 14,000 ft. during its flight to the target. The guns were designed for high accuracy, which would be far easier to achieve against fixed ground targets than that achieved by smaller caliber capital ships guns designed for use against other warships. The small number of these huge guns, like the 18-in guns designed for HMS *Furious*, were not intended to be fired in salvos.

Top: The unique Tiger Class Battlecruiser, HMS *Tiger*, trailed by the Light
Battlecruiser HMS *Renown*, punches through a heavy swell during a patrol in
North Sea. With the advent of the Renown and Courageous Classes,
Battlecruisers like the Tiger and Lion Classes began to be referred to as 'Heavy
Battlecruisers' for a short time. Above: HMS *Renown* at anchor. The location is
thought to be Scapa Flow. British Official

Top: The Light Battlecruisers HMS *Repulse* and HMS *Renown* during a turn eight points to starboard during a sortie in the North Sea during World War 1. Note the Kite Balloon above and to the rear of the rearmost vessel. Above: The Light Battlecruiser HMS *Repulse* trails behind Battlecruisers of the Invincible and or Indefatigable Class while departing the Firth of Forth on 8 April 1917. BO

Renown and *Repulse* were both laid down on 25 January 1915 (incidentally being Lord Fisher's birthday) at Fairfield Company and John Brown & Company on the Clyde respectively. *Repulse* was launched on 8 January 1916, followed by the launch of *Renown* in March that year. *Repulse* was commissioned on 18 August 1916 followed by *Renown* in September that year. Following the loss of three Battlecruisers at the battle of Jutland a few months earlier, the two ships entered service amid mixed feelings. On the one, hand their 15-in guns were more powerful than anything the enemy had afloat, but on the other hand their vulnerability to enemy shell fire was all too apparent as the lessons of the Battles of the Dogger Bank and Jutland were being absorbed.

In 1916, Captain H.F.P. Sinclair was appointed to command HMS *Repulse*, which conducted steam trials in the Clyde from 15 August 1916, gunnery trials being conducted on the 18th before she sailed for Portsmouth, achieving something in the order of 125,000 SHP during the trials. She conducted further steam trials off the Isle of Arran whilst steaming northward through the Irish Sea, attaining a speed of 31.725 knots at 118,913 SHP, although she was in excess of 3,000 tons above her normal loaded displacement.. Her design speed was then put at 32.5 knots at an output of 120,000 SHP. **Note:** Some material suggests Repulse departed the Clyde on the 18th and conducted gunnery trials the following day. Further steam trials were conducted on the 20th, before she sailed for Portsmouth, being allocated as Flagship of the 1st Battle Cruiser Squadron on 21 September 1916.

HMS *Repulse* departs her anchorage in the Firth of Forth on 8 April 1917. BO

Renown conducted contractor trials in August 1916. From late September she embarked upon acceptance trials during which she apparently attained a speed of 32.69 knots (some sources state 32.58 knots at an output of 126,300 SHP). She then moved to Scapa Flow to work up with the Grand Fleet, joining the 1st Battle Cruiser Squadron in January 1917, before she entered a short refit at Rosyth from February to 1 April 1917.

Admiralty records show that in July 1917, HMS *Repulse* was Flagship of the 1st Battle Cruiser Squadron, flying the Flag of Rear Admiral R.F. Phillimore, C.B., M.V.O., (Commanding the 1st BCS). HMS *Renown*, HMS *Princess Royal* and HMS *Tiger* made up the remainder of the Squadron.

HMS *Renown* Legend at 30 December 1914 with inputs from later Legends

Length: 750 ft. (230 m) pp; 794-ft (242 m) overall
Beam: 90-ft. (27.5 m); also stated in some documentation as 89-ft 11.5-ft.
Draught: various draft figures were produced ranging from 25 ft. forward, 26-ft. aft, 27.5 ft. (8.4 m) and 29-ft 8-in (8.94-m)
Displacement: The Legend of 30 December 1914 puts empty weight for Renown at 26,000 tons and the Legend of 22 April 1915 puts empty weight of Repulse at 26,500 tons. Weight was 31,592 tons loaded
Propulsion System: Brown Curtiss Geared turbines, four shafts delivering a design out of 112,000 SHP (83.5 MW) which was exceeded; 42 x Babcock and Wilcox large-tube boilers
Fuel capacity: 4,243 tons
Speed: 31 knots (57-km/h)
Range: 3,650 miles (5870 km)
Armour Protection: side belt 6-in (152 mm) tapering to 1.5-in (38 mm) at end; barbets 7-in (18 cm) down to 4-in (10 cm); main armament turret front faces 8-in (Repulse Legend for 22 April 1915 shows increase to 9-in (some records refer to 11-in - 30 cm), roof 4.25-in (10.8 cm); bulkheads 4-in fore (Legend for Repulse at 22 April 1915 shows 4-in fore and 3-in aft), Conning Tower 10-in (25-cm), communications tube 3-in (76 mm), torpedo fire control tower, forecastle deck 1.5-in (38 mm), upper deck 0.5-in (1.25 cm), lower deck 2.5-in (6.4 cm) in Repulse Legend of 22 April 1915, 3.5-in (9 cm) over steering compartment; main deck 2-in slope/1-in flat (some records show 3-in-76 mm), funnel uptakes sides 1.5 in and 1-in ends
Fire control: MK IV Dreyer Table and Dreyer Turret Control Table and Dreyer-Elphinstone clock.
Armament: primary armament consisted of six x 15-in/.42 (381-mm) guns in three twin turrets, two forward and one aft. Other armament consisted of 17 x 4-in/.44 (102-mm) low-angle guns; 2 x 3-in (76-mm) anti-aircraft guns; 4 x 3-pdr., and 2 x submerged 21-in torpedo tubes
Complement: 967, increased in service

Courageous Class and HMS *Furious*

The Courageous Class and the later unique HMS *Furious* have uniformly gone down in history under the rather spurious designation of Large Light Cruiser, but are continually included in descriptions of Battlecruisers. Initially the official designation of these classes of vessels was actually 'Light Battlecruiser' like the *Renown* and *Repulse* before them. *Renown* and *Repulse* only became designated as Battlecruisers after the decisions to increase their armour protection to allow them to take their place in a fleet action against enemy Battlecruisers (although they were still considered woefully inadequate in armour protection). The Courageous Class, however, retained the designation of Light Battle Cruiser and not the Large Light Cruiser designation as is all too often claimed. Even after Lord Fisher left the Admiralty in May 1915, his official documentation and letters to the Prime Minister, Royal Navy and the Admiralty, all referred to these Classes of vessels as Light Battle Cruisers. Furthermore, Lord Fisher's successor at the Admiralty also referred to them as Light Battle Cruisers in official documentation and his letters to the Prime Minister. Even the tit for tat letters to the Prime Minister from Lord Fisher and his successor over who was to blame for the lack of orders placed for Destroyers and other light craft, as well as Battlecruisers, in 1914-1915, dated 15 March 1916 and 31 March 1916 respectively, referred to the Courageous Class, HMS *Furious* and the *Renown* and *Repulse* as Light Battlecruisers. The Large Light Cruiser label was unofficially applied because the Courageous Class, unable to conduct the role required of a Battlecruiser, were allocated to Light Cruiser Squadrons before going to the 1st Cruiser Squadron. They, however, still retained the official designation of Light Battle Cruiser throughout the remainder of World War I.

In Lord Fisher's letter to the Prime Minister dated 15 March 1916, he argued against the claims that it was not possible to lay down any large ships after fulfillment of the orders placed under the previous directorship. He stated that he had instructed Camel Laird and Company to increase the length of one slip to 1,000 ft. for which he had hoped to lay down the first of a new class of fast Battlecruiser in summer 1915 (dubbed HMS *Incomparable* by Lord Fisher). He lamented the then current administration at the Admiralty by stating that the slip, which was ready in summer 1915, had lain empty since then, which to his dismay, he pointed out, was contrary to the Third Sea Lords statement that "all the large slips had been filled... and consequently no more ships of the largest size could have been laid down." Further infuriating Fisher was the fact that inquiries confirmed that other slips could be rendered suitable for capital ship building within a short period of time. The lack of new 'Heavy Battlecruisers' would place increasing importance on the Light battle Cruisers, particularly the Renown Class.

Like the Renown Class before them, completion of the Courageous and Furious Classes fell behind once Lord Fisher left the Admiralty in May 1915. In March 1916, Fisher contended that had he remained in charge of their construction then the *Courageous* and *Glorious* would have been delivered by May 1916 and the *Furious* in July 1916. He stated that they would have been laid down earlier than was the case but for the restrictions placed by the directive that no large vessels that could not be completed before the end of 1915 were to be laid down. This effectively meant that nothing larger than a Light Cruiser could be laid down after the 1914 directive communicated to the Admiralty by the then Fist Sea Lord.

The Light Battlecruiser HMS *Glorious* at anchor with another warship, probably either HMS *Repulse* or *Renown* in the background. British Official

These controversial warships were originally laid down under plans for Lord Fisher's equally controversial Baltic Project, which required some 600 or so low draught vessels capable of entering the shallow waters of the Baltic Sea to support a Russian landing on the German Pomeranian Coast, which lying only around 90 miles from Berlin, the German Capital, it was supposed would position a huge Russian Army favourably to advance and occupy Berlin, which, if the old rules of war had applied, would have led to the surrender of Germany, ending the war in 1915 or 1916; all theoretical of course.

The Baltic had long been considered the Achilles Heel of the Germanic States if it were involved in a war with Russia and another nation possessing overwhelming naval superiority; going into the 20th Century this was seen as Great Britain. In 1781, a Russian Army had seized the Baltic port of Kolberg from where it could occupy most of Pomerania where it over wintered in preparation for a spring campaign, which was not conducted as peace was signed between Russia and Prussia following the death of the Czarina.

Top: Namesake of its Class, HMS *Courageous* slips into its anchorage on its return from Scapa Flow in the Orkney Islands. Above: Destroyers of the 4th Division lead the Light Battlecruisers HMS *Courageous* and HMS *Glorious* to sea in the Firth of Forth. The *Courageous* and *Glorious* can be seen approaching for their passage beneath the Forth Rail Bridge. BO

Militarily the German Baltic coast was, arguably, its most vulnerable point during World War I. Certainly in Germany itself a variant of the Baltic Plan was feared as among the greatest threats to Germany during a war with the Triple Entente; Great Britain, France and Russia, as Germany's huge army would be committed to the Western and Eastern fronts facing the French and Russian armies respectively, leaving scarce few forces available for the defence of the Baltic coast.. With the German army so heavily committed on the Western and Eastern fronts, the main defence of this area was reliant on the German Fleet, which also had to counter the British Fleets in the North Sea and North West European coast.

HMS *Glorious* belches black smoke as she gets up steam. British Official

A tug alongside the Light Battlecruisers HMS *Glorious* as she is towed into Rosyth. The single twin 15-in gun turrets fore and aft and single funnel characterised the Courageous Class making them easy to distinguish from the Renown Class. British Official

It was concluded that for any variation of the Baltic Plan to succeed would require the commitment of the entire British Battle Fleet, which, it was equally clear, left Great Britain vulnerable to a German counterstroke; an invasion which would be practically uncontested at sea, necessitating the withdrawal from the Baltic and therefore the collapse of the entire campaign. To counter this threat of counterblow, Lord Fisher, in autumn 1914, pushed for the North Sea to be sown with thousands of mines, for which task he purchased eight fast ships to be fitted out as fast minelayers. However, the vast minefields were not sown.

In the Baltic Projects original guise, Lord Fisher envisioned the small 1914 BEF (British Expeditionary Force) of four or five Divisions being landed at Antwerp, Belgium, covered and supported by a large British Fleet (a plan drawn up in 1908) instead of being incorporated and used up as a small part of the French line as was eventually the case. Holding Antwerp would have been the firsts step to an eventual advance along the coast in conjunction with actions by the British Grand Fleet and other Fleet organisations. This would, it was hoped, have culminated in securing the coast for the Fleets advance into the Baltic to support the Russian landing on the Pomeranian Coast; all based on the assumption that the Royal Navy would be able to force its way through the formidable German North Sea and Baltic defences. Whether or not, this would have led to a defeat of Germany in 1915/16 is something that will be debated through the ages, however, one thing is clear to any professional or amateur tactician, it was certainly the only realistic chance of ending the war favorable to the Triple Entente in 1915/16. It would of course have been a very high risk strategy, but risk is after all what is required in war if victory is to be sought against an enemy of similar or superior strength to your own forces.

When Lord Fisher returned to the Admiralty as First Sea Lord on 30 October 1914, with the war less than three months old, he lobbied for support, which was forthcoming, from Lord of the Admiralty Winston Churchill and Lloyd George, then Chancellor of the Exchequer, allowing him to embark upon an ambitious building program of 612 vessels of various types that were required for the Baltic Project, which was then being referred to as an Offensive in Northern Waters.

His writings show that Lord Fisher was of the opinion, and actually tried to push as policy, for Britain not to spend huge sums raising and equipping a huge land Army for operations on the European Continent, but to apply those resources to providing an even more decisively powerful Battle Fleet, which could force its way into the Baltic and sweep the German Fleet from the Baltic Sea, clearing the way for the vast Russian Army to be landed on the Pomeranian Coast. This he stated was the only possible way of defeating Germany in 1915. The alternative course of raising and equipping a huge land Army could only bring victory after years of slaughter on both sides. Equipping this huge army also drained away the equipment and other support that Britain would have had to afford to Russia had the Baltic Project gone ahead. For Russia on its own was not in a position to provide the equipment required for such a huge undertaking as its industrial capability severely lagged behind those of its Entente partners, Britain and France, and was vastly inferior to those of its principal enemy's, the German and Austro-Hungarian Empires.

HMS *Glorious* **at anchor.** MOI

In the event, Britain was compelled to field ever more Divisions of the British Army as recruits were absorbed into Lord Kitchener's volunteer Army and sent to the Western Front, considered by many in power to be the only theatre where a decision could be reached by one side or the other. While not being outright cancelled, the Baltic plan, which, in one form or another, was a number of years old even before the start of World War I, was put on the back burner. The failures of the Dardanelle's bombardments in February and March 1915, combined with the vulnerability of Capital ships to mines and Submarines, the lesson of which was again highlighted during the Dardanelle's campaign, led to the plan being all but abandoned in official circles, and certainly never again seriously considered after spring 1915.

Although the Baltic landing plan had been dropped some vessels designed for the project were completed with some modifications, including the Courageous Class, which, as completed, were not as low in draught as they had been planned to be. However, they were certainly lower than Capital Ships of the time and this would allow then to follow German light forces retreating into shallow coastal waters, areas which had previously been off limits to heavy caliber gun ships such as Battlecruisers and Battleships.

HMS *Courageous.* British Official

Some recent claims are that the Courageous Class and the unique HMS *Furious* were not designed and built for that Special Strategic purpose, but rather built to overcome problems with Light Cruiser speeds in heavy seas, be it the North Sea or North Atlantic. However, these claims are completely without foundation and completely ignore historical records which overwhelmingly support the FACT that these vessels were designed for the 'Special Strategic Purpose'. Even long after they had been laid down Fisher's writings refer to their design and construction as being for that "Special Strategic Purpose".

In effect the Courageous Class, and more particularly with the *Furious*, it could be argued, were designed as a sort of very fast monitor, which could conduct certain Cruiser functions while armed with a Battlecruiser or Battleship main armament, although reduced in number to only four heavy caliber guns in the case of the Courageous Class and only two in the design approved for the *Furious*. In the event the *Furious* was completed with only a single 18-in gun primary armament; the forward turret being omitted and a flying off platform for the operation of aircraft being fitted in its stead. In his writings Lord Fisher stated of these warships "The "Furious" (and all her breed) was not built for Salvoes! They were built for Berlin, and that's why they drew so little water and were built so fragile, so as to weigh as little as possible, and go faster." While bombardment would have been a major role, particularly for the *Furious*, Fisher made it clear that the vessels, which were designed with powerful armament, high speed and shallow draught, were intended to protect the naval force against enemy Cruisers and light forces such as Torpedo Boat Destroyers, with their shallow draught allowing then to follow enemy Light Cruisers into shallow coastal waters, thus removing their previous safe sanctuary from the guns of capital chips as stated above. This latter role was not only planned for operations in the Baltic Project, but was also planned for the German North Sea Coast, where Light Cruisers could use their high speed to escape capital ships and head to the sanctuary of shallow coastal waters.

Of the 18-in guns designed for HMS *Furious*, Lord Fisher wrote in 1919 "…with their enormous shells were built to make it impossible for the Germans to prevent the Russian Millions from landing on the Pomeranian Coast!." Impossible may have been a strong word, but the 18-in guns would certainly have been welcomed as invaluable support to any landing force had the Baltic Project been carried through to fruition.

HMS *Furious* on the starboard side of May Island in the Forth Estuary. BO

The Courageous Class design, the legend of which was officially submitted by the DNC (Department of Naval Construction) for approval on 28 January 1915, resembled that of a reduced size Renown Class, armed with four 15-in guns in two twin turrets as opposed to the six guns in three turrets of the Renown Class; the 'A' turret position of the Renown design being omitted for the Courageous Class; the reduction in main armament turrets to only two giving the Class an unmistakable profile compared to the *Renown* and *Repulse* as deletion of the forward most turret took away the superimposed forward two turret appearance that had bestowed every British Battlecruiser designed since HMS *Lion*. The armour protection suite was basically that of a Light Cruiser, with the exception of the main armament turrets and barbets. This lack of armour protection was the main obstacle to their being considered capable of taking their place in the line of battle during a fleet engagement.

Previous page and this page top: HMS *Furious* arrives in the Firth of Forth on commissioning. Above: The *Furious*, with attendant Destroyer escort, during her work up in the Firth of Forth on 4 July 1917. As completed, the *Furious* was armed with a single 18-in gun mounted in 'Y' turret as her heavy armament, the planned forward turret being omitted in favour of a flying off platform and accommodation for aircraft. British Official

Of the Courageous Class, Fisher's successor at the Admiralty stated in March 1916 that these were "ill named vessels" and "They are not battle cruisers – light or heavy. They possess no effective armour." However, he did contend that their designation was indeed Light Battle Cruiser despite their inability to conduct many of the tasks associated with Battlecruiser operations.

Even at the early design stage there was much criticism of the poor armour protection in the vessels, which were in effect planned to go into service as Capital Ships. In early March 1915, when it was becoming clear that the Baltic Project was unlikely to ever be approved. Eustace Tennyson d'Eyncourt was ordered by Lord Fisher to modify the designs by increasing the thickness of the torpedo protection bulkheads, not only in the Courageous Class, but also the 0.75-in bulkheads in *Renown* and *Repulse*. This modification would result in a considerable weight increase in all vessels concerned with the added expense of increasing the draught, which in the case of the Courageous Class, effectively ended any hopes of them being completed with a shallow enough draught to enable them to operate as planned in the 'Special Purpose' Baltic Operation; no real catastrophe in the Admiralty's eyes as this plan had been all but shelved.

As they were still on the drawing board the modifications to the Courageous Class was relatively straightforward to implement, with the bulkheads increased in thickness from 0.75-in to 1.5-in for an increase in overall design weight of 500 tons, but more damaging, considering their original design role, was the increase in draught by 6-in. The reductions in speed caused by the increased weight and deeper draught were relatively modest at only 0.25 knots. When notified of the increase in weight and draught, Fisher simply replied that this would have to be accepted in order to increase the underwater protection against torpedoes and mines. This fact indicates that even before they had been laid down, Fisher no longer saw the primary role of the Courageous Class as being to operate in the shallow coastal waters of the Baltic. This was rounded upon by Lord Fisher's successor who said in a letter to the Prime Minister in early 1916 "They were built says Lord Fisher, for a 'special strategically purpose,' though I may incidentally observe that owing to their draught, this 'strategically purpose' is one which they will never be able to fulfill.

The planned increase in bulkhead thickness for the *Renown* and *Repulse* was eventually abandoned as the ships were so advanced in their construction that the modifications were deemed to impose a considerable, and unacceptable, delay in their completion dates.

The design changes for the Courageous Class were officially approved by Lord Fisher on 14 March 1915, paving the way for the first of the two ships, HMS *Courageous*, to be laid down at Elswick on the Tyne on 28 March 1915, followed by the *Glorious*, which was laid down at Harland & Wolff, Belfast, on 20 April 1915. By this time it was becoming clear that the Baltic Project was unlikely to be seriously considered following the failures at the Dardanelles earlier that year.

Top: HMS *Furious* during her work up in the Forth Estuary. Above: HMS *Furious* with a Tug alongside her in the Firth of Forth. British Official

In March 1916, Lord Fisher wrote to the Prime Minister stating that although designed for this 'Special Strategic Purpose' the ships would be useful addictions to the fleet despite no longer being required for the purpose for which they were designed. Fisher stated, "These vessels were designed and built for a special strategic purpose, but nevertheless they will be extremely valuable for general work with the Grand Fleet. It is not necessary to go into details, but in my opinion they will be worth a great number of Light Cruisers and Destroyers to the Commander-in-Chief, both before and during a general action." He went on to say "They were never intended to replace heavy battle cruisers of the 'Lion' type and it is merely obscuring the issue to discuss them from that point of view. They are supplementary to such ships. The same applies in less degree to the 'Renown' and 'Repulse'. It may or may not be the case that more heavy battle cruisers are required, but this has no connection whatever with the building of these light battle cruisers."

Courageous was launched in February 1916, followed by *Glorious* in April that year. HMS *Glorious* commenced trials on 23 October 1916. She conducted steam trials in the Irish Sea off the Isle of Arran in December 1916, during which she apparently attained a speed of 31.42 knots at an output of 91,195 SHP. *Courageous* conducted a series of limited trials on 16 November 1916 in the area of the mouth of the River Tyne, during which she apparently reached 30.8 knots at an output of 91,200 SHP. If she could attain an output of 110,000 SHP then speed was estimated to be 33 knots.

In January 1917, HMS *Glorious* commissioned as Flagship of the 1st Light Cruiser Squadron (this would lead historians to appoint the fallacious Large Light Cruiser label). *Courageous* commissioned into the 3rd Light Cruiser Squadron) in January 1917. The *Courageous* and *Glorious* would eventually be used to reconstitute the 1st Cruiser Squadron, which suffered severe losses at the Battle of Jutland on 31 May 1916.

HMS *Courageous* had her first real brush with the enemy in April 1917 when she was attacked by Submarine U-43, which had departed Germany for a patrol in Irish waters on 8 April 1917. U-43 sank several vessels; one of her victims being the *Woodward Abrahams*, a US sailing vessel of 744 toms which was inbound to Liverpool from Pensacola in the US. At 7.10 pm., the *Woodward Abrahams* was stopped by U-43 in position 51° 23'N. 19° 50' W., some "400 miles west (true) from the Fastnet". The *Woodward Abrahams* was abandoned and sunk by bombs. U-43 now turned onto an eastward course where she encountered HMS *Courageous* in position 51° N. 18° W. the following morning, 23 April, at 9.00 am. She fired two torpedoes, which missed, passing astern of *Courageous*, which had departed Plymouth on 21 April, bound for Scapa Flow, escorted out by two Destroyers.

There are many dates put forward from various records for the *Courageous* and *Glorious* joining the 1st Cruiser Squadron, but it appears that the earliest credible dates would be the end of July 1917. The Admiralty Squadrons and Flotillas from War Vessels and Air Craft, Monthly Return for July 1917 shows that in that month HMS *Courageous* was Flagship of the 3rd Light Cruiser Squadron flying the Flag of Rear-Admiral T.D.W. Napier, C.B., M.V.O. The remainder of the squadron consisted of HMS *Glorious*, HMS *Furious* and the Light Cruisers, HMS *Birkenhead*, *Chester*, *Yarmouth* and *Chatham*.

HMS *Glorious* fitted with a flying off platform on her fore turret. British Official

Courageous Class Legend at 28 January 1915 and inputs from later Legends
Length: 735-ft pp (225-m)
Beam: 80-ft, increased to 81-ft (24.7-m) before construction began
Draught: 21-ft 9-in mean or 23.25-ft
Displacement: 17,400 tons (increased to stated 17,800 tons, although armour protection modifications were actually closer to 500 tons, which should have increased displacement to 17,900 tons and weight was further increased in service following sea trials with figures as high as 18,600 tons being quoted and even Admiralty writings of early 1916 stating weights of 19,000 tons).
Machinery: Parsons all-geared steam turbines producing 90,000 SHP
Speed: 32 knots
Range: 6,000 nm at a speed of 20 knots
Fuel Oil: 750 tons standard and 3,250 tons maximum
Armament: main battery of 4 x 15-in guns (80 rounds per gun - rpg), 16 x 4-in guns (120 rpg), 3 x 3-in HA (High Angle) anti-aircraft guns (150 rpg), 5 x Maxim machine guns (5,000 rpg), 2 x 21-in Torpedo Tubes ((10 x Torpedoes)
Armour suite: side belt 3-in (7.6-cm) amidships tapering to 2-in (5-cm) forward, barbets 7-in (18-cm) down to 3-in (7.6-cm), main armament turret front faces reported as 13-in, later 9-in, turret sides 11-in and tops 7-in, bulkheads 2-in forward and 2.5-in aft, Conning Tower 10-in (25-cm) thickest, communications tube 4-in down to 3-in, torpedo fire control tower 3-in, main deck 0.75-in flat, equivalent to 1-in sloped, forecastle deck 1-in (2.5-cm), lower deck 1-in forward and 1.5 (3.8-cm) to 3-in aft, upper 1-in (2.5-cm), torpedo bulkheads 0.75-in, funnel uptakes 0.75-in
Complement: 842, increased in service

The fire control system for the Courageous Class consisted of a Dreyer/Elphinstone clock Barr and Stroud 15-ft. (4.6-m) rangefinder. The electronic communications gear consisted of Types 1-6 Wireless sets.

HMS *Furious* berthed, probably during fitting out. BO

HMS Furious
Length: 735-ft pp (225-m)
Beam: 88-ft
Draught: 21-ft 6-in mean
Displacement: 19,200 tons
Machinery: Brown-Curtis geared steam turbines, SHP: 90,000 - 94,000 SHP
Speed: 31.5 knots
Range: 6,000 nm at a speed of 20 knots
Fuel Oil: 750 tons standard
Armament: planned main battery of 2 x 18-in guns (only 1 actually fitted), 8 x 5-in, 3 x 3-in HA (High Angle) anti-aircraft guns (150 rpg), 5 x Maxim machine guns (5,000 rpg), 2 x 21-in Torpedo Tubes (10 x 21-in Torpedoes carried)
Armour suite: side belt 3-in (7.6-cm) amidships tapering to 2-in (5-cm) forward, barbets 7-in (18-cm) and 6-in down to 3-in (7.6-cm), main armament turret front faces 9-in, turret sides 5-in, bulkheads 3-in - 2-in fore and 3-in aft, Conning Tower 10-in (25-cm) thickest, communications tube 3-in, torpedo fire control tower 3-in, main deck 0.75-in flat, equivalent to 1-in sloped, forecastle deck 1-in (2.5-cm), lower deck 1-in forward and 1.5 (3.8-cm) to 3-in aft, upper 1-in (2.5-cm), torpedo bulkheads 0.75-in, funnel uptakes 0.75-in
Complement: Just under 900 as a quasi-aircraft carrier

3

THE SECOND BATTLE OF HELIGOLAND BIGHT – 17 NOVEMBER 1917

The action known as the second battle of Heligoland Bight originated when the German High Seas Fleet initiated a plan to gather information about the huge British minefields and nets located outside the main German line of mines in the Horns Reef-Terschelling area of the Heligoland Bight near the main German High Seas Fleet bases. The German fleet required to know the areas covered by the prolific British mine laying with a view to establishing routes out into the North Sea which would avoid the main mine belts. A number of so called "Test trips" would be carried out, each being major operations in their own right, involving vessels to detect mines, minesweepers followed by Torpedo Boats, U-Boats, Barrier Breakers and Light Cruisers for protection, all supported by Sea Planes for scouting ahead, providing information on British warships. The groups conducting the "Test trips" were protected by heavy warships only on routes that were known to be mine free.

For the British, the laying of extensive minefields had become one of its main pre-occupations in its defensive measures to protect its sea lines of communications and trade routes. The minefields were designed to bottle up, or at least make movement difficult for German U-boats and surface raiders; the threat posed by the latter being driven home hard in October 1917 when two modern German Light Cruisers, SMS *Brummer* and SMS *Bremse* (both had joined the High Seas Fleet in 1916 and were armed with a 150-mm gun main battery) sailed with orders to attack shipping in the British convoy route between Lerwick in the Scottish Shetland Islands and Bergen in Norway. The German warships reached the convoy route during the night of 16-17 October, lying in wait for a convoy they had been alerted to by radio traffic.

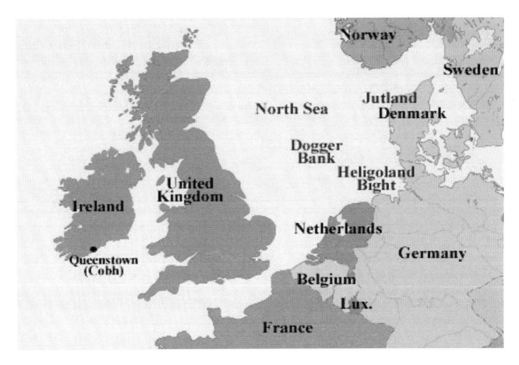

Map of the British Isles, North West Europe and the North Sea showing the positions of Jutland, Dogger Bank and Heligoland Bight, the principal areas of Battlecruiser actions in home waters, including the action of 17 November 1917 in the area of Heligoland Bight. UK NA

The German official documentation records that there were ten Merchant ships escorted by two or three Destroyers, but the British Admiralty records show that there were actually twelve Merchant ships escorted by two Destroyers, HMS *Mary Rose* and HMS *Strongbow*, with the latter at the head of the convoy, which was inbound to Lerwick from Bergen, sailing in double row formation. Before dawn on the morning of 17 October, the German Cruisers sighted the convoy some 61 miles from the Shetland Islands and moved to engage while the lead British Destroyer, HMS *Strongbow*, immediately headed for the German ships in a valiant effort to protect the convoy. The German account records the *Strongbow's* attack on the Cruisers, but records that the other Destroyer, HMS *Mary, Rose*, steamed off to the North. *Strongbow* was quickly sunk by the overwhelming firepower of the German Light Cruisers, which then turned to the Merchant ships, which according to German records, had stopped and the crews lowered boats. Before the Light Cruisers could sink the Merchant ships HMS *Mary Rose* returned and attacked them, but like the *Strongbow* before, she was quickly sunk by the overwhelming firepower of the German vessels, which then went on to sink ten of the Merchant ships. Only 10 men from HMS *Mary Rose* survived while 47 crew from the *Strongbow* were lost.

Royal Navy Light Cruisers and Battlecruisers, including HMS *Inflexible*, attempted to intercept the German Cruisers after the attack, but failed to locate the German ships which were heading back to the sanctuary of their base after their successful attack. HMS *Inflexible* took on-board the survivors from the Destroyer *Mary Rose*.

In early November 1917, a Large Convoy transiting form Norway to Scotland was covered by a powerful Royal Navy Escort which included Battleships and Light Cruisers to provide a protection force more powerful than any anticipated raiding force.

November 1917 had begun with a success for the Royal Navy when a Squadron of Light Cruisers accompanied by Destroyers engaged and sunk the German Auxiliary warship *Kronprinz Wilhelm*. Ten German Trawlers were also sunk during this sweep.

During the week ending 11 November 1917 a Battlecruiser Squadron accompanied by Light Cruisers and Destroyers conducted a sweep in the North Sea, "Skirting the minefields in the Heligoland Bight." No enemy vessels were encountered.

The Germans planned for one of the 'Test Trip' operations on 17 November 1917, with a force comprising the 2nd and 6th Auxiliary Mine Sweeper Half Flotilla's, 12th and 14th Torpedo Boat Half Flotilla's, Barrier Breaking Division IV and Light Cruisers from Scouting Group Division II, all under the overall command of Rear-Admiral Von Reuter from the 6th Mine Sweeper Half Flotilla. Elements of Squadron IV, consisting of the Battleships SMS *Kaiser* and SMS *Kaiserin*, under the command of Captain Grasshof in *Kaiserin*, were to act as covering force for the group. These two powerful Dreadnought battleships, each armed with a main battery of ten x 12-in guns, were detailed to lay off a point west of Heligoland by 07.00 am when the "Test-trip" group assembled in its designated area of operations in the Heligoland about the centre off Horns Reef-Terschelling. Unable to get airship scouts and with the Light Cruisers unable to embark Sea Planes, the German force relied on land based Sea Planes from Borkum, an Island in lower Saxony, off North west Germany, for scouting ahead of the group, with two aircraft sent out on patrols.

Just after 08.00 am, the German Minesweepers came under fire from the British Light Cruisers HMS *Caledon* and HMS *Calypso*, two Caledon group of 'C' Class Light Cruisers, each with a main battery of five x 6-in guns and a maximum design speed of 29 knots. It is recorded that the German Light Cruisers SMS *Konigsberg* and SMS *Nurnberg* moved towards the British cruisers on a N.W. course in order to protect the Mine Sweepers, while the Torpedo Boats of the 12th and 14th Half Flotilla's moved North and N.W. in order to lay down a smoke screen between the Mine Sweepers and the British Warships, although Torpedo Boat V45, finding itself in a favourable position, launched a torpedo attack on the British ships while the Mine Sweepers retired on an East course behind the smoke screen. An account emanating from the German side states that when the British Light Cruisers opened fire on the Mine Sweepers the Flagship of Scouting Group II, SMS *Konigsberg*, had left to close up the 2nd and 6th Mine Sweeping Half Flotilla's, therefore, the Light Cruiser SMS *Nurnberg* (Captain Hildebrand) moved on a course N.W. to provide protection for the Mine Sweepers, which, quite naturally, would be forced to retire in the face of the British Light Cruisers. The German Torpedo Boats moved to the North and North West in order to lay down the smoke screen between the Mine Sweepers and the British warships. With the withdrawal of the Mine Sweepers in progress the German Torpedo Boats and Light Cruisers altered course to the south east, laying more smoke as they withdrew, positioning themselves between the British Cruisers and the German Mine Sweepers.

The British Light Cruisers then switched their attention from the Mine Sweepers to the more inviting target of the German Light Cruisers, but, due to the immense smoke that had been laid down by the German ships, were 'obliged' to bear down on the southern wing of the German formation (to windward) of the German Cruisers which would allow the British ships a better opportunity of observing the German ships and enable them to fire more accurately.

The official German account states that the British Large ships (the Battlecruisers) did not progress beyond the "windward edge of the smokescreen" because of the threat of mines, obliging them to try and remain within the water that the German Light Cruisers had passed through.

Eventually the German Light Cruiser were receiving the attention of not only the British Light Cruisers and the *Courageous* and *Glorious*, but also the 15-in guns of HMS *Repulse*, with several salvo's landing within their formation, which was following a zig-zag course. The German account claims that at 09.24 am the German Light Cruisers attained hits on two of the British Battlecruisers and that the Light Cruiser SMS *Pillau* hit a British Destroyer several times forcing it to sheer off and withdraw from the battle. Post war documents show that the German were steaming at full speed with the aim of trying to pull themselves and the British Light Forces away from the British Battlecruisers in order that they could then attack the British Light Forces. However, they were dismayed to note that the Battlecruisers were easily staying with the smaller ships due to their very high speeds, which in the case of the *Repulse, Renown, Courageous* and *Glorious* was actually higher than most of the Light Cruisers on both sides.

The German U-Boats from the Auxiliary Mine Sweeping Half Flotilla's had been on a course E.S.E, and at 08.50 am., they were engaged by a northern group of British Destroyers. They again claimed to have come under fire from around 09.05 to 09.30 am before they returned to port. The northern British group of Destroyers also made contact with the vessels of the German 6th Mine Sweeping Half Flotilla, but no hits were attained and the Mine Sweepers returned to port, without the Destroyers following up their attack. Prior to this the Mine Sweepers had again been in the vicinity of the German Light Cruiser, which were also retiring ahead of the British warships. The Light Cruisers SMS *Nurnberg* and the *Pillau* laid down more smoke to conceal the Mine Sweepers, aided by further smoke from the 14th Torpedo Boat Half-Flotilla. According to the German account this had the effect of causing the British Destroyers (which by that time were very close) to turn away from the smoke and allowed the German Mine Sweepers to withdraw on an E.S.E course. A Post war German account stated that it was possible that the British Destroyer commanders thought the smoke to be poison gas being the reason for turning away. However, for such an action to have occurred it is far more probable that the British suspected that the smoke was being laid to conceal mines, which the German Torpedo Boats and Light Cruisers may have lain in their path.

Around 09.50 am., British Destroyers apparently launched an unsuccessful torpedo attack against German vessels, followed by an equally unsuccessful torpedo attack launched against British ships by the German Torpedo Boats, with six torpedoes being launched from the German Torpedo Boats and further torpedoes also being launched unsuccessfully from the Light Cruisers SMS *Konigsberg* and SMS *Frankfurt*.

At 10.30 am, the German Light Cruisers observed the two German Battleships SMS *Kaiserin* and SMS *Kaiser* under Admiral Von Reuter who held his ships steaming on an easterly course in the hope of tempting the British Light Cruisers and Battlecruisers to pursue him right through the various British and German minefields, also placing the British ships between the German Battleships and Light Cruisers, leaving the British only avenues of retreat to either the north or north-west through belts of mines. Now the German Battleships altered course to the N.W. due to misinterpretation of signals from the Light Cruiser SMS *Konigsberg*, heading straight for the ships involved in the ongoing battle. The German Light Cruisers now undertook to join up with the two German Battleships which had by now opened fire, engaging the British Light Cruisers, with a hit being observed on the leading British Light Cruiser, which, together with the other British Light Cruisers turned away in the face of the overwhelming German firepower. The British ships, however, continued forcing, and when the German Battleships and Light Cruisers turned to pursue them a shell hit the Light Cruiser SMS *Konigsberg* causing a serious fire to break out in her bunker. This was apparently the last shot fired in the action, the German side claiming that the British then broke off and withdrew, the British claim that the Germans were withdrawing and they would not pursue them owing to the danger of mines.

By this time the two German Battlecruisers SMS *Hindenburg* and *Moltke* had appeared on the scene, giving the Germans four powerful Battleships and Battlecruisers, which although they carried less powerful guns than the British Battlecruisers, they carried more heavy guns than their British counterparts and their ships were much better protected. The British Light Battlecruisers HMS *Repulse* and *Renown* were little better protected than an obsolete Armoured Cruiser while the *Glorious* and *Courageous* were protected by an armour suite little better than that of a Light Cruiser, except in the case of their main armament turrets and barbets, as recounted in the previous chapter. Only HMS *Tiger* was considered a Heavy Battlecruiser capable of taking its place in the line of battle against German Heavy Battlecruisers like the *Moltke* and *Hindenburg*, but it would not have been wise for even the *Tiger*, which in any case was much further to the rear, to engage in a line of battle action with the German Battleships. The huge advantage that the British Battlecruisers had over the German heavy ships was their superior speed, allowing then to decide whether battle would be joined or not. In this respect Admiral Fisher could claim that the much criticised Light Battlecruisers had proved their worth by engaging the German units allowing the British Light Cruisers to retire and then breaking off when conditions did not favour them. On the other hand critics of the Light Battlecruisers, of whom there were many, could claim that the lack of armour protection dictated that the British Light Battlecruisers had no real choice other than to break off the engagement when faced with heavily armoured German Battleships and Battlecruisers.

In the course of the battle the Germans claimed five hits on British Battlecruisers (British records show no hits being received on any of the Battlecruisers – Light Battlecruisers), six hits on Light Cruisers and seven hits on destroyers. British records show that the Light Cruiser HMS *Caledon* was the only British ship to receive any significant damage, being hit twice, at least one of which was by a heavy calibre shell from a German Battleship. Other ships suffered superficial damage including the Light Cruiser HMS *Calypso* which suffered two hits and the Light Cruiser HMS *Cardiff* which was hit five times.
German documents confirm three hits by 15 cm shells and two hits by heavy shells on their Light Cruisers, one of which hit the *Konigsberg*, passing through all three of the ships funnels before penetrating the upper deck and into a coal bunker before exploding against the bunkers inner wall causing a fire, but otherwise very little damage, due probably to the protection afforded by the coal bunker. Fragments from this shell were confirmed by German analysis that it was 15-in (38 cm), which was the first actual German confirmation that the Royal Navy now operated Battlecruisers armed with this caliber main armament.
German records state that the "outpost" Steamer *Kedingen* was captured by the British. This vessel had been positioned as mark-sip at the Test-trip start line. German records claim that this vessel was engaged by 15-in gunfire from the Battlecruisers before being captured in an undamaged condition after the crew had abandoned ship.
Admiralty records claimed that one of the German Mine Sweepers in the first group was sunk, then a vessel in the second group blew up after being hit

by fire from the Cruisers before the other German vessels in this group disappeared. The third group then, according, to Admiralty records, turned south and was immediately pursued by the 1st Light Cruiser Squadron, which exchanged fire with this group in "a running engagement taking place under a heavy smoke screen until within 30 miles of Heligoland, when four enemy Battleships were sighted ahead and opened fire, hitting the '*Caledon*' aft with a heavy shell." By this time Admiralty records claim that one of the German Light Cruisers was "heavily on fire", while another appeared to be heavily damaged, suffering from much reduced speed. Admiralty records also claim that a third German Light Cruiser suffered a "violent explosion" when it was hit by the last salvo of 15-in shells fired from HMS *Repulse*, which along with HMS *Renown*, *Courageous*, *Glorious* and *Tiger*, had followed up the 1st Light Cruiser Squadron. It is probable that the heavy German smoke screens gave the impression on the British that ships were being damaged and fires started.

British personnel losses were 22 killed and 43 wounded with 21 Germans killed and 40 wounded. Materially the battle was a defeat for the Germans as they lost a minesweeper and suffered damage to a Light Cruiser, while the British suffered damage to some Light Cruisers. However, that is not the way battles should be judged. The Germans could also claim victory as they had successfully protected the bulk of their Mine Sweepers; a single minesweeper being the only vessel sunk during the engagement.

Post battle the German Command doubted reports from the German Light Cruisers that the Courageous Class Light Battlecruisers had only two main armament turrets, one fore and one aft. This first engagement with the Light Battlecruisers of the Renown and Courageous Classes left the Commander of the German High Seas Fleet, Admiral Scheer, with an enviable impression of their extremely high speed in comparison to previous generation ships. He also claimed post war that the engagement left him with the impression that this high speed had been attained at the price of much reduced armour protection, a conclusion he came to after being informed that the British Battlecruisers were reluctant to advance significantly against the fire of the German Light Cruisers, something which would have been brushed aside by a heavily armoured ship.

As best as can be ascertained, from records on both sides, the wind was blowing at force 2-3 from W.N.W. with a slight swell in the sea. The western horizon was covered in sea mist, but the eastern horizon appeared clearer giving the British an advantage in observing at least the type of vessels being engaged.

As can be seen with critical examination between records on both German and British sides and eyewitness accounts, it is clearly shown that the fallacious engagement between HMS *Repulse* and the two German Battleships which is often claimed in various writings did not actually take place.

Note: Some writings record the Light Battlecruiser, HMS *Courageous* as opening fire at 07.37 am, however, the most reliable British and German records suggest, strongly, that the first vessels to open fire were the Light Cruisers HMS *Caledon* and HMS *Calypso*, which commenced firing just after 08.00 am.

Records are sparse and often contradictory, but it appears that the Light Battlecruisers that engaged the German warships fired several tens of 15-in shells, one account claiming Courageous fired just over 90. About half an hour or so into the action Glorious apparently had one gun out of action in her forward turret due to a mishap not attributed to enemy action

Admiralty Official Communiqué

On November 17th during a reconnaissance of the Heligoland Bight our Light Cruisers sighted three groups of enemy vessels steering to North-Westward. The first group consisted of ten minesweeping vessels and destroyers, followed by a second group consisting of five to eight craft resembling submarines, three of which appeared to be very large and to have funnels. This force was followed by a third group consisting of at least four light cruisers and a number of destroyers.

Fire was opened immediately and one vessel of the first group, a minesweeper, was sunk before the group disappeared to the North-East in a smoke screen.

A lucky shot caused a heavy explosion in and apparently destroyed a vessel of the second group, whereupon the other vessels of this group disappeared.

The third group turned to the South-east, pursued by the First Light Cruiser Squadron, the Sixth Light Cruiser Squadron and the First Cruiser Squadron, a running engagement taking place under a heavy smoke screen until within 30 miles of Heligoland, when four enemy battleships were sighted ahead and opened fire, hitting the "Caledon" aft with a heavy shell.

One enemy cruiser was seen to be heavily on fire, a second was badly damaged and reduced in speed, and a violent explosion was caused in a third by the last salvo from the battle cruiser "Repulse," which had followed up our light cruisers.

The damage to our ships was superficial except in the "Caladon" which was hit twice; "Calypso" also was hit twice, and Cardiff about five times. All ships engaged are ready for service, except the "Caledon." Our total casualties were 1 officer and 21 men killed, and 4 officers and 39 men wounded. We picked up 22 prisoners.

The following letter is stated in Lord Fisher's Writings to have come from a high ranking naval officer present at the Second Battle of Heligoland Bight on 17 November 1917:

December 12th, 1917.

Dear Lord Fisher,

In the late action in the Heligoland Bight the only heavy ships which could get up with the enemy were the "Repulse," "Courageous" and "Glorious" (the "Renown" and "Furious" were elsewhere). They very nearly brought off an important coup! Without them our light cruisers would not have had a "look in," or perhaps would have been "done in!" When public speakers desired to decry the work of the board of which you were a Member in 1914 and 1915, and particularly that part of the work for which you were so personally responsible as this new type of heavy ship, no condemnation was too heavy to heap upon your design!

It is a pleasure to me, therefore, to be able to let you know that they have fully justified your anticipation of their success.

Top: HMS *Glorious* and HMS *Repulse* at the Grand Fleet's main anchorage, Scapa Flow in the Orkney Islands. Above: HMS *Repulse*. The Light Battlecruisers were the only Royal Navy Capital Ships to become involved in the action known as the 2nd Battle of Heligoland Bight. BO

Top: The Light Cruiser HMS *Calypso* was hit twice during the course of the battle. Above: The appearance of two German Dreadnought Battleships, including SMS *Kaiser* (above) which engaged the British Light Cruisers, inflicting some damage on HMS *Caledon* which was hit by a 12-in shell.

4

POSTSCRIPT

During the remainder of the war the Light Battlecruisers operated in the North Sea with the British Grand Fleet to keep the German High Seas Fleet bottled up and to intercept same if it put to sea on mass. There were few notable incidents, one such being when HMS *Repulse* was involved in a collision with HMAS *Australia* on 12 December 1917; *Australia* requiring three weeks or so in dock for repairs to be carried out.

In 1918, HMS *Renown* was part of a British raiding force in the Kattegat, again in an attempt to entice the German High Seas Fleet to respond. However, again the Royal Navies efforts were frustrated as no major German forces sailed to intercept the British. On 6 March 1918, the 1st and 2nd BCS's and their attendant Destroyers covered a mine-laying operation.

In October 1918, *Renown* conducted trials with flying-off platforms for aircraft fitted to 'B' and 'Y' turrets. *Renown, Repulse, Courageous* and *Glorious* sailed with the Grand Fleet to accept the surrender of the German High Seas Fleet on 21 November 1918. *Repulse* entered into an extensive refit on 17 December 1918, just over a month after the Armistice took effect. In April 1919, *Renown* joined the Battle Cruiser Squadron of the Atlantic Fleet.

HMS *Furious* joined the Grand Fleet based at Scapa Flow after commissioning on 4 July 1917, and working up in the Firth of Forth. She was never a fully-fledged Light Battlecruiser, but was completed as a quasi-aircraft carrier, operating as an aircraft carrier during 1917-18. On 19 July 1918, the *Furious* was the centerpiece of a force which sailed to conduct a carrier air strike on the Zeppelin sheds at Tondern Schleswig. The covering force for this historic carrier air strike was the five Revenge Class Battleships of the 1st Division, 1st Battle Squadron of the Grand Fleet, 1st and 7th Light Cruiser Squadrons, all screened by Destroyers, with the entire force placed under the overall command of Admiral Sir Charles Madden, flying his flag in the 15-in gun Battleship HMS *Revenge*. The raid was the highlight of her wartime career, but she survived the post war fleet reductions and commenced conversion into a fully fledge straight through deck aircraft carrier in 1922.

In 1918 *Courageous* was part of the 1st Cruiser Squadron. In 1919 she was allocated as Gunnery Training Ship at Portsmouth and joined the Reserve Fleet in 1921, remaining until takin in hand to be converted to an aircraft carrier in 1924. *Glorious* was moved to the Reserve Fleet at Rosyth on 1 February 1919, and, like her sister, was eventually taken in hand to be converted to an aircraft carrier.

All five of the Light Battlecruisers went on to serve in World War II, *Courageous*, *Glorious* and *Furious* as aircraft carriers; *Courageous* and *Glorious* being sunk during that war. *Repulse* and *Renown* served as Battlecruisers, the latter surviving the war while, the former was sunk, along with the King George the V Class Battleship, HMS Prince of Wales, by Japanese bombers off the coast of Malaya on 10 December 1941.

APPENDICES

Appendix I

Principal British Squadrons, Flotillas and Warships that participated in the Second Battle of Heligoland Bight on 17 November 1917

1st Battle Cruiser Squadron

HMS *Lion* (Battle Cruiser Force Flagship flying the Flag of Vice-Admiral Sir W.C. Pakenham, K.C.B., K.C.V.O., Commanding B.C.F.)

HMS *Repulse*, Flagship of 1st BCS flying the flag of Rear Admiral Richard F. Phillimore, C.B., M.V.O., Commanding 1st BCS) – Captain William H.D. Boyle
HMS *Renown* (her log and letters from Senior Officers would suggest, strongly, that Renown was not present. She appears to have been docked at Rosyth at the time of the engagement).
HMS *Princess Royal*
HMS *Tiger*
HMS New Zealand – Some documents show the *New Zealand* attached to the 1st BCS, although, like the Battlecruisers of the Lion and Tiger Classes, she was not involved in the action of 17 November 1917
Note: Only HMS *Repulse* became involved in the Battle, the other Battlecruisers being well out of range, providing distant cover for the eventuality that German heavy units would pursue the British Light forces.

The 1st BCS was screened by elements of the 13th Destroyer Flotilla - the Light Cruiser HMS *Champion* (Flotilla Leader) and the Destroyers HMS *Verdun*, HMS *Telemachus*, HMS *Oriana*, HMS *Nepean*, HMS *Obdurate*, HMS *Tristram*, HMS *Petard* and HMS *Tower*

1st Cruiser Squadron

HMS *Courageous* (Flagship of 1st Cruiser Squadron flying the flag of Vice Admiral Trevvlyan D.W. Napier) - Captain Arthur Bromely
HMS *Glorious* - Captain Charles B. Miller C.B.

Destroyers of 13th Flotilla attached to screen the 1st Cruiser Squadron

HMS *Ursa*, HMS *Nerissa*, HMS *Urchin* and HMS *Umpire*

6th Light Cruiser Squadron

In the Admiralty Squadrons and Flotillas from War Vessels and Air Craft, Monthly Return for July 1917 the squadron consisted of HMS *Cardiff* (Flagship Rear Admiral Edwyn S. Alexander-Sinclair C.B. M.V.O.; appointed on 11 July 1917) - Captain Claud H. Sinclair, HMS *Ceres*, HMS *Calypso*, HMS *Caradoc* and HMS *Cassandra*. Of these the *Cardiff* (Flagship), *Calypso*, *Caradoc* and *Ceres* participated in the action of 17 November 1917, screened by the Destroyers HMS *Valentine*, HMS *Vimiera*, HMS *Vanquisher* and HMS *Vehement*

1st Light Cruiser Squadron

In the Admiralty Squadrons and Flotillas from War Vessels and Air Craft, Monthly Return for July 1917 the squadron consisted of HMS *Caledon* (Flagship Commodore Walter H. Cowan C.B., M.V.O., and D.S.O.), HMS *Cordelia*, HMS *Galatea*, HMS *Inconstant* and HMS *Phaeton*. HMS *Caledon* (Flagship), HMS *Galatea*, HMS *Inconstant*, and apparently joined by HMS *Royalist*, participated in the action of 17 November 1917, screened by the Destroyers HMS *Vendetta* and HMS *Medway* of the 13th Flotilla

1st Battle Squadron –provided distant cover

In the Admiralty Squadrons and Flotillas from War Vessels and Air Craft, Monthly Return for July 1917 the squadron consisted of the Battleships HMS *Revenge* (Flagship), HMS *Benbow*, HMS *Marlborough*, HMS *Royal Oak*, HMS *Canada*, HMS *Resolution*, HMS *Royal Sovereign*, HMS *Iron Duke* and the Light Cruiser *HMS Blonde*. Several vessels of the 1st Battle Squadron, with its attendant Destroyer screen, provided distant support for the Operation

Appendix II

Principal German Squadrons, Flotillas and Warships that participated in the Second Battle of Heligoland Bight on 17 November 1917

Under the overall command of Rear-Admiral Von Reuter

6th Mine Sweeper Half Flotilla
2nd Auxiliary Mine Sweeper Half Flotilla
6th Auxiliary Mine Sweeper Half Flotilla
12th Torpedo Boat Half Flotilla
14th Torpedo Boat Half Flotilla
Barrier Breaking Division IV

Light Cruisers from Scouting Group Division II

SMS *Konigsberg*, SMS *Nurnberg*, SMS *Pillau* and SMS *Frankfurt*

Covering Force under the command of Captain Grasshof in the Battleship SMS *Kaiserin*

Elements of Squadron IV consisting of the Battleships: SMS *Kaiserin* and SMS *Kaiser*

Outpost Steamer Kedingen

Battlecruisers

SMS *Hindenburg* and SMS *Moltke*
Note: the German Battlecruisers arrived at the end of the battle and did not participate

Appendix III

Grand Fleet Strength March 1917

Battleships
HMS *Iron Duke* (Fleet Flagship)

1st Battle Squadron	9 Battleships
2nd Battle Squadron	9 Battleships
4th Battle Squadron	9 Battleships
5th Battle Squadron	4 Battleships (15-in guns and a speed of 25 knots)

Battle Cruiser Fleet (renamed Battle Cruiser Force later in the year)

HMS *Lion* (Flagship)
1st Battle Cruiser Squadron	4 Battle Cruisers
2nd Battle Cruiser Squadron	4 Battle Cruisers
2nd Cruiser Squadron	5 Armoured Cruisers
1st Light Cruiser Squadron	4
2nd Light Cruiser Squadron	5
3rd Light Cruiser Squadron	6
4th Light Cruiser Squadron	6
5th Light Cruiser Squadron	8
6th Light Cruiser Squadron	1
Light Cruisers attached to Battle Squadrons	4
Light Cruisers attacked to Destroyer Flotillas	3
Light Cruisers attacked to Submarine Flotillas	1
Flotilla Leaders	12
11th Destroyer Flotilla	18
12th Destroyer Flotilla	18
13th Destroyer Flotilla	26
14th Destroyer Flotilla	18
15th Destroyer Flotilla	18
Destroyers attacked to Submarine Flotillas	4

HMS *Queen Elizabeth* — 15-in gun battleship with a speed of 25 knots. She was allocated as Grand Fleet Flagship later in the year

The above mentioned vessels constituted the main strength of the Grand Fleet, which faced the German High Seas Fleet in March 1917. There were also large number of vessels in home waters, which were not a part of the Grand Fleet, these being employed on various tasks. This included the Battleship HMS *Dreadnought* and five Pre-Dreadnought Battleships of the King Edward VII Class, which were based on River Thames as an anti-invasion measure.

Appendix IV

British appreciation of the strength of the German High Seas Fleet in March 1917

Battleships

SMS *Baden* (Fleet Flagship)
1st Squadron (consisting of 4 Battleships of Heligoland Class and 4 of Nassau Class
3rdSquadron (consisting of 1 Battleship of the Bayern Class and 4 of the Konig Class)
2nd Squadron (consisting of 7 Pre-Dreadnought Class Battleships)

Battle Cruisers

SMS Derfflinger, SMS *Seydlitz*, SMS *Moltke* and SMS *Von der Tann* for a total of four operational

There was considered to be thirteen Light Cruisers operational with the High Seas Fleet. As well as large numbers of Torpedo Boat Destroyers.

Note: Submarine strength for both fleets has been omitted in the above appendices

GLOSSARY

BCS	Battle Cruiser Squadron
BEF	British Expeditionary Force
BO	British Official
cm.	Centimetre
CS	Cruiser Squadron
DNC	Department of Naval Construction
ESE	East South East
ft.	Feet
HA	High Angle
HMAS	His Majesty's Australian Ship
HMS	His Majesty's Ship
IJN	Imperial Japanese Navy
in.	Inch
LCS	Light Cruiser Squadron
LOC	Library of Congress
m.	Metre
MOI	Ministry of Information
NW	North West
RAN	Royal Australian Navy
RN	Royal Navy
rpg.	Rounds per Gun
SHP	Short Horse Power
WNW	West North West

BIBLIOGRAPHY

Main Documents Consulted

War Cabinet 469A

Battle Cruiser Strength. Memorandum for the War Cabinet., dated 20 August 1917

Battle Cruiser Position and Ship-Building Program, Admiralty Memorandum for the War Cabinet

Letter from Lord Fisher to the Prime Minister, dated 18 February 1916 and 15 March 1916 respectively

H.S. 410/716

Records of Warship Construction during the War, 1914-1918, D.N.C. Department, 1919

Admiralty Squadrons and Flotillas from War Vessels and Air Craft, Monthly Return for July 1917

HMS *Barham* Log, August 1916

Admiralty Official Communique for the action of 17 November 1917

M. 05268/17

The High Seas Fleet in World War One

Records by Admiral of the Fleet, Lord Fisher

British Naval Policy, Memorandum for the War Cabinet, July 1917

A General Review of the Naval Situation, Memorandum for the War Cabinet, 24 March 1917

A General Review of the Naval Situation, April 1917 – June 1918, Memorandum for the War Cabinet

Letter from the First Sea Lord, 17 April 1917

SECRET G-66, Naval Situation, Letter from Lord Fisher to the Prime Minister, March 1916

SECRET G-58, Observations by the First Lord of the Admiralty on the Prime Ministers Note (G-57) on Naval Policy dated 22nd February 1916

SECRET G-86, Report on Recent Naval Affairs, October 1916

Naval Weekly Appreciation No.22

Naval Weekly Appreciation No.23

Naval Weekly Appreciation No.24

Naval Weekly Appreciation No.25

Naval Weekly Appreciation No.26

Various Ship Legends for HMS Renown, Repulse, Courageous, Glorious and Furious

British Battlecruisers of World War 1, an Operational Log', 2013

I addition many miscellaneous papers and letters, political, industrial and naval were consulted

ABOUT THE AUTHOR

Hugh, a historian and author, has published in excess of forty books; non-fiction and fiction, writing under his given name as well as utilising two different pseudonyms. He has also written for several international magazines, whilst his work has been used as reference for many other projects ranging from the aviation industry, international news corporations and film media to encyclopedias, museum exhibits and the computer gaming industry. He currently resides in his native Scotland

Other titles by the Author include
British Battlecruisers of World War 1 - Operational Log, July 1914-June 1915
Hurricane IIB Combat Log - 151 Wing RAF, North Russia 1941
RAF Meteor Jet Fighters in World War II, an Operational Log
Typhoon IA/B Combat Log - Operation Jubilee, August 1942
Defiant MK.I Combat Log - Fighter Command, May-September 1940
Blenheim MK.IF Combat Log - Fighter Command Day Fighter Sweeps/Night
Interceptions - September 1939 - June 194
Tomahawk I/II Combat Log - European Theatre - 1941-42
Fortress MK.I Combat Log – Bomber Command High Altitude Bombing
Operations, July-September 1941
Eurofighter Typhoon - Storm over Europe
Tornado F.2/F.3 Air Defence Variant
Air to Air Missile Directory
Boeing X-36 Tailless Agility Flight Research Aircraft
X-32 - The Boeing Joint Strike Fighter
X-35 - Progenitor to the F-35 Lightning II
X-45 Uninhabited Combat Air Vehicle
North American F-108 Rapier
Sukhoi Su-34 'Fullback' – Russia's 21st Century Striker
F-84 Thunderjet - Republic Thunder
USAF Jet Powered Fighters - XP-59-XF-85
XF-92 - Convairs Arrow
The Battle Cruiser Fleet at Jutland
Saab Gripen, The Nordic Myth
Dassault Rafale, The Gallic Squall
Boeing Super Hornet & Growler - F/A-18E/F - EA-18G

13949630R00042

Printed in Great Britain
by Amazon.co.uk, Ltd.,
Marston Gate.